Let None Walk Alone

Let None Walk Alone

Sister Juanita Ujcik, *OSF*

*a guide for family and friends
of incarcerated people*

Mid-Atlantic Highlands

Mid-Atlantic Highlands
Huntington, West Virginia

Printed in the United States of America

Book and cover design: Mark S. Phillips
Editorial coordination: Ace Boggess
Cover photograph: Sr. Marianne Saieg
Illustrations: Debbie Richardson

ISBN-13: 978-0-9864267-6-6 (Softcover)

Mid-Atlantic Highlands
An imprint of Publishers Place, Inc.
821 4th Ave. Suite 201
Huntington, West Virginia 25701
www.publishersplace.org

Contents

DEDICATION

For the Incarcerated, Their Family and Friends
who shared their WALK and their STORIES
For Stanley and Mary Ujcik
who taught me to WALK in many ways
For the Sisters of St. Francis of Mary Immaculate
who have always WALKED with me on the Journey

THANKS to

Publisher John Patrick Grace who shares the call and the WALK

Editor Ace Boggess who knows the WALK and put it all together

Sr. Vivian Whitehead, my mentor, and all the Sisters for support & wisdom

Staff of Center for Correctional Concerns and JUST of DuPage for work & ideas

Renee Cipriani for practical guidance

Sr. Helen Prejean for her leadership and encouragement

Sr. Marianne Saieg, the photographer, the Artists, Readers, Colleagues, Family & Friends for patience, stories & inspiration

FOREWORD

LET NONE WALK ALONE IS A "Thank you" to those who desire to walk faithfully with the incarcerated. It is a guidebook for those who are early or late in the walk with a person facing an experience in jail, court and more. It is both an affirmation and a vessel of ideas for the journey of many years that some must endure. It encourages one's gift of support, understanding, patience, creativity, and especially presence over the months and years of incarceration.

As someone who has invested her life to serve men and women on death row and elsewhere in prison, I am overjoyed to recommend Sister Juanita Ujcik's compassionate book.

She wrote it, out of her thirty years plus of prison ministry experience, for the people most hurt and ignored by incarceration: the families. This book will be a lifesaver for them and will inspire them to more creative ways to help their loved ones behind bars, whether in jail or in prison.

LET NONE WALK ALONE shows family and friends of those indicted and/or convicted of crimes how to accompany their loved one through the long trek of trial, sentencing, incarceration and even, eventually, release back home. The book provides information, strategies, resources and common sense. In short, it is a gem.

Sister Juanita and I want you, the families and close friends, to know that you do not walk alone. God's grace and God's servants are with you every step.

For professionals—chaplains, counselors, correctional officers—this book can add useful information and deepen your understanding of the family's point of view and concept. It should also help you to encourage and direct their efforts to support rehabilitation through loving letters, calls and visits..

Those still in educational settings, internships and training will find a brief concise, comprehensive view of what occurs in courts, jails and prisons and in many instances, the reasons for what happens.

Churches and other religious organizations that extend their ministries into prison and jail settings, such as Kairos, Prison Fellowship, Yokefellows and other kindred groups, should all discover in this book a valuable aid.

Because each person is unique, each state and institution has its own laws, policies and practices, and since every situation is different, our presentation is an overview of the system. It sketches a variety of reasons and responses to events that occur, on the street, in the courtroom, and in penal institutions.

This book believes that we can all reach out to each other in our own way. Those incarcerated, our families, others in similar situations need us to make a difference in their lives.

As I once wrote elsewhere, Let us lavish love on others.

Receive love gratefully when it comes to us, cultivate friendship like a garden, for it is the best love of all.

Sister Helen Prejean, CSJ
Author: *Dead Man Walking: An Eyewitness Account of the Death Penalty In the United States*

Introduction

DON'T TELL AUNT MARY

AUNT MARY WAS THE YOUNGEST of eight children — a single branch on a family tree larger than a California Redwood. She came into the world a year after one of her nephews — Chuck — making her an aunt from the day she was born. Now, having lived into her 90s, Mary had a family with more than 300 members. She knew all of them, even the most distant cousins and spouses. She stayed in contact with them by sending cards, making phone calls, and passing along details of their joys and sorrows. Because of this, some considered her a busybody who loved nothing more than a little juicy gossip. The truth, however, was that she cared about her family and wanted to keep everyone close by sharing information.

One day, Mary's friend Liz called and told her about a name she read in that morning's newspaper. "Isn't that your brother-in-law?" she asked. It wasn't. Instead, it was Phil — one of Mary's great-nephews. He had been arrested and charged with a drug crime.

So, Mary phoned her niece Joyce, Phil's aunt. Joyce didn't know anything about it, so she in turn called her sister Charlotte, Phil's mother.

Charlotte said her son was in trouble with the law, and he would be spending time in prison. "I feel so bad," she said. "He's the first in our family to be arrested."

Phil wasn't the first. Had Aunt Mary been asked, she could've named most of the family members with a criminal record, even those going back several generations.

Still, for Charlotte, this was something new and quite a shock. She felt fear and anger, along with a lot of embarrassment. She didn't want anyone else to hear about her son's troubles. The last thing she said to Joyce was, "Don't tell Aunt Mary." How surprised she would have been to find out that Aunt Mary was the first to know.

This is the big secret that is no secret at all. Most criminal cases—at least the felonies—are covered in the daily newspapers where anyone can read about them. In the age of the internet and with the rise of social media, keeping anything like this under wraps is almost impossible. Even without the old and new media, however, when people disappear for a number of years, their absence will be noticed. Questions surface. Speculation grows.

Americans often talk about serious issues like this. Discussions take place on television news programs, in the pages of the daily papers, in political debates, and on social media sites. Calls will be made to reform the justice system, to eliminate mandatory sentencing guidelines, or to place drug offenders into treatment programs rather than jail. Yet, that's the public face. On a more personal, individual level, many folks never feel comfortable talking about such things—even with those close to them—especially when a family member is involved. That can lead to problems and misunderstandings. People attempting to keep secrets often isolate themselves, thereby suffering alone because they have no one to help them with their burdens. They feel increasing levels of tension and anxiety in company, while building resentment toward the incarcerated loved one. Some grow angry with the prisoner, many with the system, others with themselves or God, whatever their religion. Some become so upset that they lash out at people they know, or else hold their feelings in until they become sick themselves. Marriages break up, families divide, and friendships of many years are lost.

The best way for these family members to regain peace of mind is for them to be open about whatever has happened, no matter how seemingly bleak, and share their stories. Talking with others can relieve the tension and stress, calm the growing anger, and sometimes provide a new understanding of incarcerated people and the struggles they must have gone through to end up where they are.

True, there will be judgmental folks who criticize and are quick to place blame. Others might listen with precision so they have information to share when trading gossip. Nonetheless, those close friends and family members who genuinely care will offer their support and provide assistance no matter what crime might be involved or how long the person must spend behind bars. Friends show their true colors when their friends are stuck in a crisis.

After all, having a family member locked up is not uncommon today. In the U.S., about one out of every 32 people will interact with the criminal justice system at some point, while one out of 100 actually will face incarceration. On any given day, there are more than two million people behind bars in the United States. They come from both sexes, all races, religions and economic backgrounds. They live in the city, the suburbs, and rural areas. These people have parents, spouses or significant others, children, siblings, and friends. In addition, their actions have affected their neighbors and coworkers, their victims and their victims' families, the taxpayers, as well as all police officers, lawyers and judges involved in the case. In other words, everyone is in some way connected with a person serving time in prison or jail.

In the example above, Aunt Mary understood this. She currently was corresponding with another nephew doing time. She could have eased Charlotte's grief by showing how Phil wasn't the only one in the family and how his trespasses were small. Charlotte shouldn't have said, "Don't tell Aunt Mary." Instead, she should've asked for Mary's help.

WHY THIS BOOK IS NEEDED

My work in jails and prisons began as an educator and led to my becoming a director. When you are directing anything, you have to make all the difficult calls. In my first couple of years, I worked mainly with residents and observed the pressures and difficulties they faced. Then my job expanded to include social service and making contact with families. The more I spoke with parents, spouses, significant others, siblings, etc., the more my understanding of their side of the problem was enhanced. The fear and helplessness in their voices showed me how much of a mess the uncertainty made of their lives. They felt isolation and had an unwillingness to talk about their incarcerated loved ones. I watched them and recognized the patterns that developed. My staff and I gave them the information they needed. Sometimes we even offered suggestions for future situations they might face.

Early in my jail work, I began looking for books for those families. A few outside groups had prepared pamphlets and information sheets, but those were local in nature and often limited to a single piece of the puzzle. My colleagues and I created a list of these materials we could share with both the residents and their families. Through the years, this local list grew larger and larger. However, there was still no book.

Later, I joined the National Convocation of Jail and Prison Ministry and traveled yearly to meetings around the country. I thought that perhaps I might find a book from another organization that would serve the families. That turned out not to be the case.

When Kairos Outside Illinois—a retreat program for women with incarcerated relatives—was started, several people, including the Bishop of Joliet, mentioned me by name as someone that should be involved. I joined the group and worked a dozen weekends, plus several more with Kairos Outside Indiana, usually serving as spiritual director. I met many brave and self-sacrificing women during that time. Some of these women were direct victims of crimes. All were dealing with life while their relatives and other loved ones were trapped behind prison walls. They often were reluctant to talk with anyone, but in time they were able to share in these special groups of women with similar stories. I learned many things from them about struggles, difficulties and successes.

As the years went on, I continued searching for that special book that would make a difference in the lives of these families. It needed to explain the criminal justice system in detailed but understandable terms. It should reassure family members that their actions were supportive and good. At the same time, it would have to remind them that success or failure of someone on the inside might be beyond their control, while teaching them how to cope with either eventuality. Of course, there was no such book.

MY JOURNEY TO WRITING THIS BOOK

Joliet is a prison town. The sisters in my religious community have provided ministry, education, service, and support to inmates since before 1900. I lived in the area as a child, but did not plan to become involved in this ministry. I had reached middle age when I began to work in a jail.

In order to describe the world of jails and prisons to those that haven't experienced it, a writer needs to develop an in-depth understanding of not only the process but also the day-to-day realities of incarceration. I encountered folks from all walks of life and shared their sufferings. I've seen the inside workings of jails and prisons. This knowledge needs to be passed along. My intent is to make the situation as easy as possible for those coming face to face with situations related to the criminal justice system. Now it's a matter of getting this information on paper.

As for me, the first time I met someone who had been incarcerated, I was seven or eight years old. I didn't know this about him beforehand, or even what it meant that he had been to prison. Such concepts were strange and scary to a child.

From time to time, my family traveled to visit relatives in other states. On one such excursion, we stopped to see an elderly couple. They were neighbors once, and part of my grandparents' generation. My father went to school with their sons, and our families had been friends for many years. We visited the couple before, and both seemed like sweet, decent people. This time, my dad warned us about the husband, whom he described as *not a nice guy*.

I soon saw what my father meant. The couple had a beautiful garden, and all of us, including the husband, went outside to look at it. While we were there, the man's dog got in his way. He brutally kicked the animal as if it were a football.

In the car, while we were on our way home, my mom turned to my father and said, "Now I see what you mean."

Only then did my dad tell us more about the man. He said the guy had beaten his sons without mercy when they were children. Also, he had purchased hotels and burned them down for the insurance money. For that crime, he was caught and spent several years in prison.

That was my first encounter with someone who had been incarcerated. It alarmed me. I, like most of society, assumed all criminals were as cruel and deceitful.

Still, my parents lived by a philosophy that became a part of my reality. They used to say, "You're not better than anybody, and nobody's better than you." They had a free spirit and eclectic tastes. They took me to sporting events, plays, concerts, religious festivals, tractor pulls, county fairs and art exhibits. I met a wide variety of people over the years and learned that what my parents said to me was true. It helped me keep an open mind later on.

A few years after I saw that man kick his dog, a police officer wrote a traffic citation to one of my uncles for the offense of not stopping at a stop sign. My uncle lived miles away and was visiting our small town, so he asked my mother to pay the fine for him. Mom agreed. Then she and I stopped by the local police station to take care of the ticket.

Inside that tiny station, I saw a holding cell. It had bars like those shown in old movies, and it looked menacing and uncomfortable. This seemed like a different world to me—a nightmare where the monsters were kept behind cage doors that were locked shut but just as easily might open.

When I enrolled at the College of St. Francis (now the University of St. Francis) and entered the convent, I was 18 years old. That was in the early 1960s (John Kennedy served as President of the United States, and Dr. Martin Luther King Jr. worked for racial justice), and the College of St. Francis offered a liberal-arts program that fit in well with the times. I graduated in four years.

My first teaching position was with second-grade students. I don't know how much they learned from me, but they taught me a lot. Whereas older kids pretend they know what you are saying even when they miss the point altogether, younger children just stare at you with blank expressions on their faces. So, that year I began to adjust my vocabulary to fit my audience.

I taught at high schools after that and took graduate-level courses in different subjects at various universities, earning my Master's Degree from Rensselaer Polytechnic Institute in Troy, N.Y. I enjoyed teaching and knew I did a good job.

After the murder of Dr. Martin Luther King Jr. and chaos and devastation from riots that followed, I began to think differently about my role as a teacher. To me, education was one key to changing our country. I made the choice to teach in the inner city and received permission from my community. There were no open positions in the schools where we were established, so I found a job in the public schools. For the next 15 years, I taught in a primarily African-American high school in Ohio.

My first run-in with the law happened at that school. I was part of the teacher's union. Each high school had a committee of eight elected members, with one of them serving as the union steward. One year I was nominated to the committee, forgot to remove my name and was elected. Our steward found another job soon after, and I was asked to take over the role. As luck would have it, three weeks later the teacher's union went on strike. We picketed for 17 days. I did my part as steward, running the strike from my car.

Ohio, at the time, had laws stating that public employees couldn't strike. We'd broken the law and, in response, the Court issued several arrest warrants for strikers from our school. I was the steward, so my name appeared on one of those warrants. I'm still not sure what the actual charge was. Of course, it turned out to be a formality. None of us were arrested, and all the charges went away after the strike ended. Still, I came a bit too close to spending time in jail. That taught me a lesson: *anyone, even a Sister, can run afoul of the law and wind up behind bars.*

After teaching in public school for 15 years, I decided to return to the Joliet area to be near my parents. By that time, Sister Vivian Whitehead had started the Center for Correctional Concerns (CCC) at the local jail. Now she offered me a job.

Located in the basement of the Courthouse, the jail could best be described as a dungeon. It had traditional bars rather than the metal doors used more often today. Its walls were concrete. Each tiny cell housed a number of inmates because the jail, built for 70 people, was already overcrowded by half that number. All cells contained bunk beds, a shower, and a toilet. Each dayroom—the area shared by all inmates in a cellblock or pod—was little more than a large space with a few picnic tables where the inmates sat, ate, and played cards. The pods, like cells themselves, were then separated from the rest of the jail by another gate, followed by long, winding corridors. Sounds echoed off the concrete walls, and the place was always noisy. Back then, the prisoners could smoke, so the air was thick and smelled stale like the rooms in old hotels.

I worked in the classroom, which was about 12 square feet and lined on both sides with file cabinets. Six arm-chair desks barely fit in the small space, and once they were in, moving about became almost impossible. A closet was used for one-on-one conferences.

Needless to say, I learned a great deal about the criminal justice system during those years, and even more about the people I met inside the jailhouse walls. Most residents had substance abuse issues, whether involving drugs or alcohol. Many were mentally ill. Veterans, especially, had problems related to what these days has come to be called PTSD (Post Traumatic Stress Disorder). I saw how families of these inmates were often at a loss as to how to help them.

During that time, I began to participate in the National Convocation of Jail and Prison Ministry (NCJPM), an organization intended to assist individuals involved in ministering to the incarcerated. The NCJPM met in various cities across the country, with a local chapter planning the program around a topic of interest to its specific area. For all of us involved, we gained contacts in many states, insights into successful programs and shared problems, different views from professionals in all areas of the criminal justice system, and the support that came from not feeling we were alone in what we were trying to do.

After two years, the Bishop of Joliet asked those of us at the Center for Correctional Concerns to spread our work to other counties in the diocese. For my part, I went to the new jail in DuPage County, where I started JUST (*Jail, Understanding, Serving, Teaching*) of DuPage, a similar agency with the same goals of educating inmates and assisting them with their transition back into society.

Working in a jail is never easy. The administrators keep a close watch and typically don't trust outside organizations or volunteers. They have seen folks bend or break the law before by bringing in contraband, getting involved in an inmate's case, taking mail to post, delivering messages or items to an inmate's friends or family, and becoming intimate or even sexual with a prisoner. It makes the administrators and correctional officers suspicious, and rightly so. This sort of thing happens a lot more than an outsider might suspect. So, there are rules to be followed, some of which seem absurd, but all of them in response to one bad act or another by a visitor on the premises.

With it so difficult just to get volunteers inside the jailhouse walls, our organization tried to accomplish as much as we could while there. We provided educational programs and services. We assisted people with different backgrounds, religions, levels of incarceration, and types of crimes, doing our best to meet the needs of each. Most of our work with the families was accomplished over the telephone. We helped them to make contact, explained the rules, and generally tried to show them that they weren't alone.

Another two years passed, and then I returned to my original county and took over as director of the Center for Correctional Concerns. There, I experienced the move from the old dungeon to a new state-of-the-art facility. The pods were bigger, and correctional officers were present. The officers had been trained to stop problems before anything serious happened. It made things quieter, while allowing for fewer altercations among the inmates.

In the new facility, there was a monthly management meeting with the warden. It involved the managers of various programs, including among them custodial, medical, and food services. It was during these meetings when I learned much about the operation of jails and the reasons behind many of the rules and decisions that were made, most having to do with funding, use of staff, or the types of inmates involved.

That is just a sampling of the world I came to know during my time working with inmates and their families. Most of the people I met in jail were folks who made poor choices or were caught up in serious addictions. Many had low self-esteem, leaving them unable to think clearly or positively about their lives and actions. Several refused to believe they could change, so they convinced themselves that they didn't want to in order to avoid failing again. I watched as some made parole or discharged their sentences and went on to positive futures, while others continued their cycle of bad choices and ended up right back inside. Regardless of the inmates and their paths in later life, I always tried to look for the good in them, even those who kept it hidden.

The truth is that all of us, for whatever reason, will at some point need to remove ourselves from the past and start again. When we do, we will be much better off if we have the support and care of others. Sometimes, that requires a great deal of patience and understanding.

What I share with you is a combination of my stories and those of many incarcerated people and their families, along with my staff and colleagues who have interacted with the system. If a story seems to be yours, it is only because there are many patterns and similarities in cases along with common outcomes. Most names and many crimes and circumstances have been changed for the sake of those involved.

My goal in writing this book is to provide some of that understanding for families and friends of inmates. I hope the insights offered will allow you to travel this difficult road and know that you are not alone.

Part I.
Off to Jail

RALPH'S ARREST

OWEN AND ADDIE WERE ENJOYING an evening at home. They made dinner, shared a bottle of wine, and were sitting down to watch a late movie when the phone rang. Addie answered and heard a computerized recording informing her that this was a collect call from her son, Ralph, at the local jail. Addie, already shaking and anxious, pressed one to accept the charge. It was the beginning of a nightmare.

"I've been arrested," Ralph told his parents. "It's a big mistake! I didn't do anything." When he calmed down a bit, he added, "I have a bond hearing tomorrow. Can you come and bail me out?"

For Owen and Addie, this was a shock but not a surprise. Ralph had been distant, argumentative, and hard to live with for months now. While he lived at home in a room upstairs, he rarely slept there. When he was home, he stayed in that room and kept the door closed. As if that weren't enough, he didn't have a job and already had flunked out of school. He burned incense and played his music on full volume. He rarely spoke to his parents, even to say hello. Although Owen and Addie tried to communicate with him and set down house rules, Ralph paid little attention.

Owen and Addie loved Ralph, but their responses to the call from jail were different. Addie's reaction was to say, "Quick, we've got to get him out. He's our son." Owen, on the other hand, replied, "No, we'll just let him sit for a while. The boy needs to learn to be responsible for his actions. Besides, we don't have all the facts yet, and even if we did, we couldn't do anything until tomorrow." Then, softening his stance a little, Owen added, "You know we don't have much money saved, but maybe what we do have could be used to hire a good lawyer."

That began a discussion, bordering on an argument. It lasted all evening. When the two of them went to bed, both were angry and frustrated with the situation, as well as with each other.

While Owen and Addie had mixed emotions about Ralph, he was still their son. They loved him and didn't want to see him suffer if they could help it. However, they didn't foresee his long and difficult road ahead. They couldn't anticipate all it would cost them: time, money, friends, a few family relationships, and eventually their marriage.

Ralph's arrest was this family's first contact with the criminal justice system. It would not be the last. Owen and Addie learned more than they could have wanted about jails, guards, courts, lawyers, and judges. They spent many hours in waiting rooms or standing in long lines. They went to the courthouse and listened to every mean thing the prosecutor said about their son. When they finally secured his release on bond, they tried to get him treatment for an addiction to drugs — an addiction they knew nothing about before Ralph's arrest. They did the best they could in a difficult situation.

If you are reading this book, in all probability something like what happened to Owen and Addie has happened to you. Perhaps you saw it coming, or perhaps it caught you by surprise. Either way, you've felt the same shock and concern as the couple described above. You probably experience waves

of fear and sadness, maybe even guilt, and likely a great deal
of anger. Above all, there is the uncertainty. "How could this
have happened?" you ask, and also, "What's going to happen
now?" What you need most is more information.

With Ralph and the charges he faces, details will come
out over time. Many of them will be revealed in court during
various preliminary hearings and the eventual trial. Even
then, it is important to remember that facts in most cases are
subjective based on which side tells the tale. There will be
Ralph's version as expressed by his lawyer, and the victim's
version told by the prosecutor for the state or commonwealth.
Unless Ralph enters a guilty plea, the two versions might
never come together, and a jury will be forced to reconcile
them. Even then, juries sometimes get it wrong.

How does this help you with the case of your friend or
loved one? It doesn't. It's merely a way of saying you should
take a deep breath and steady yourself for the reality that the
truth might never be clear. In the end, you will have to decide
what you do and don't believe, not to mention how much it
matters in the way you respond to your loved one.

DEALING WITH THE MEDIA

One thing that might make your situation more difficult is
coverage in the media. While sensational cases tend to dominate
the national news, on the local news, almost every felony has its
moment in the spotlight, perhaps drawing a lot more coverage
if the crime is serious or so bizarre it has entertainment value
for the viewing audience. If a man is arrested for drunken
driving after crashing his car into to the neighbor's swimming

pool, for example, it might receive more play on the TV news than a minor shooting in a downtown bar.

The same is true with newspapers. The bigger the story, or the more interesting, then the more coverage it will receive. The main difference with newspapers as opposed to television news is that reporters in the print media tend to delve deeply into a story in an effort to present more than just the bare-bones facts. However, the level of play a story receives in a newspaper also depends on the size of the paper involved. A woman arrested for stabbing her husband might be front-page news in a small-town daily paper, but in *The New York Times*, it might not merit more than a paragraph hidden somewhere in the back.

Aside from the newspapers and TV broadcasts, there also will be coverage on the internet. Friends of both the person arrested and any alleged victims are likely to post news of the incident on their Facebook and Twitter accounts. These postings have the potential to spread and reach a wider audience made up of people that might not know you or your incarcerated loved one. Moreover, while it's the nature of all media to get some information wrong, this has proven especially true for social media.

Many families of those arrested find it best to tune out all the noise of the media. That prevents some embarrassment and anger. However, if you choose to read the stories and watch the local news, try to do so objectively without getting caught up in the commentaries and bombastic dramatization.

Of course, if the crime alleged against a person is sensational enough, you as a friend or family member might find yourself in the spotlight, too. Reporters will call you or knock on your door, sometimes with a camera in tow. They want to get more details about the case, as well as something quotable from you and any display of emotions you might show. This puts you in a difficult situation.

The first thing to remember is that, under the First Amendment to the United States Constitution, reporters do have the right to approach you and ask their questions, then to quote anything you say to them in the newspaper or on television, even if you say, "No comment." However, that doesn't mean you are compelled to answer. Before you to decide to speak to the press, there are several questions you should ask yourself:

• *Is this in the best interest of the person under arrest?* Remember that other people such as the police and the prosecutor are listening. They read the newspapers and watch the TV news, too. Information that seems trivial to you might be used by a prosecutor as evidence at trial or even lead to further criminal charges. In Ralph's case, for example, should Owen mention the incense and loud music, a clever prosecutor might seize on that as evidence of Ralph's drug use. Both Owen and Addie might be called to testify at trial. Furthermore, the police might use it as probable cause to acquire a warrant to search the family home.

• *Where are you emotionally, and can you handle this?* Having a breakdown on live TV helps no one, and might add to the sense of shame and embarrassment you already feel. At the same time, if you come across as cold and aloof, it might appear to viewers that you know the person under arrest is guilty.

• *If you answer one question, will it lead to others you prefer not to discuss?* Reporters, like the police, are trained to ask questions escalating in importance. They might start out with simple, sympathetic questions about how you feel or what you believe about the person's guilt or innocence, but inevitably they will get harder, delving into things you would not want mentioned in public, possibly even some that allege your culpability—whether actual or emotional—in the person's crimes.

• *Who should speak to the media?* In Ralph's case, it might be Owen, who has a stern disposition and won't allow the reporters to take advantage of him. Or it might be Addie who best can show her love for the person under arrest. The couple might decide to hire a spokesperson to talk to the press— someone more capable of tailoring words so that nothing is taken out of context. Those are all possibilities. Even so, the best response might be for Owen and Addie to let Ralph's lawyer do all the talking.

• *To which media should you respond?* Perhaps Owen and Addie know and are on good terms with Timothy, a reporter down at the local weekly newspaper. If so, he might be more friendly than Jeff, the crusading correspondent from Channel 6. Or, maybe Owen and Addie believe their son has been framed, and a crusader is what they want. One thing to keep in mind is that the media often feed off of one another. So, once one place picks up the story, all the rest will, too.

THE ARREST

If an officer witnesses a crime (sees someone breaking into a house, for example, or watches a drug deal take place) then an arrest can be made immediately. If not, as in most cases, the process becomes more complicated.

After a crime occurs, or is alleged to have occurred, the police begin an investigation. This involves collecting evidence and taking witness statements. All of this information is gathered for the purpose of identifying a suspect with enough certainty to establish probable cause for an arrest. Probable cause is the standard. It doesn't mean the person arrested is guilty, just that enough evidence exists to take the next step in the process: acquiring a warrant for arrest.

If someone you know has been arrested, you will hear the term 'probable cause' mentioned frequently as the process moves forward. It has different meanings at every step, so it is important to try to understand the phrase, which comes from the Fourth Amendment to the United States Constitution:

The right of the people to be secure in their persons, houses, papers, and effects, against unreasonable searches and seizures, shall not be violated, and no Warrants shall issue, but upon probable cause, supported by Oath or affirmation, and particularly describing the place to be searched, and the persons or things to be seized.

In general, it refers to a reasonable suspicion supported by circumstances or evidence enough to make the average person believe that what is suspected is true. Mere suspicion is not enough. At least some evidence has to be presented.

You will hear *probable cause* mentioned in the following ways:

1) An officer decides to "stop and frisk" a person on the street.
   (*"He looked like he had a gun in his waistband."*)

2) An officer searches a vehicle during a traffic stop.
   (*"I smelled marijuana."*)

3) An officer enters a dwelling without a warrant.
   (*"I heard screams and thought her life was in danger."*)

4) An officer asks a judge to issue a search warrant.
   (*"My confidential informant said the drugs are in the basement."*)

5) A judge issues a warrant for arrest.
   (*"There's enough evidence to charge the crime."*)

6) At the initial appearance (arraignment hearing).
   (*"There's enough evidence to hold the defendant for trial."*)

7) At the preliminary hearing.
   (*"There's enough evidence to bind this case over to the Grand Jury."*)

8) At the Grand Jury proceeding.
   (*"There's enough evidence to issue an indictment."*)

As you can see, the amount of evidence required for each step of the process is a little larger. Because of that, it might seem confusing. However, the probable-cause standard is critical to every case because it is the Constitutional standard. As such, every officer, prosecutor, and judge involved must make certain the standard is applied in order to prevent a higher court from overturning the case later on.

So, once the probable-cause standard is met, only then are charges filed. That means a person officially has been accused of having committed the crime and, in all likelihood, taken into custody. If no arrest has been made, a warrant for arrest will be issued and the person charged will be picked up by the police at the earliest opportunity.

Another thing to keep in mind after a friend or loved one has been arrested is that there might be multiple charges for one crime. Consider that during a traffic stop for a broken taillight, an officer also might issue a citation for failure to wear a seatbelt, not having insurance, or texting while driving. The same thing occurs during the commission of a crime. A person arrested for armed robbery after holding up a convenience store might also be charged with brandishing a firearm or perhaps conspiracy if two or more people are involved. It is also a common tactic for police to add a charge of resisting arrest, regardless of whether a person actually offered resistance. The reasons police and prosecutors will stack charges like that are 1) to pressure the person into pleading guilty to one charge in order to avoid the possibility of being convicted for all of them, 2) to ensure at least one charge will hold up should the case go to trial, and 3) to use as leverage when convincing a person to provide information about other criminals.

This is just the beginning of the case. At this point in the process, there is no need for you to be concerned about multiple charges. Some will be dropped by the prosecutor, others rejected by the Grand Jury, and most discarded in any plea bargain struck between the prosecutor and the defendant. Likewise, additional charges might be added as new information becomes available.

JAIL

Unless you are present at the time of a loved one's arrest, the first you hear of it likely will be a telephone call from jail— probably an automated message asking if you wish to accept the charges. Calls on jailhouse phones are often limited to ten or fifteen minutes, not allowing a new inmate much time to provide you with all necessary details. This can be unnerving. The brevity and lack of information can add to what stress you feel and increase the anxiety that began to build the moment you heard the word *jail*. Even so, remember that however you feel about the person under arrest, he or she feels much worse at the moment.

Ask folks who have been locked up, and they are likely to tell you that their time in jail was the hardest thing they went through. Jail is not a nice place to be. It is a maximum-security facility designed to house three types of inmates: 1) those under arrest who have not yet made bond or been convicted of a crime; 2) those convicted of misdemeanors, serving out their comparatively short sentences (in most cases less than year); and 3) convicted felons either awaiting transfer to the penitentiary or having returned from there to await further court proceedings. The three types of inmates are housed in sections of the jail designated for each.

Keeping the types of inmates separate is meant to protect them. However, this only works to a certain extent (that is, by keeping a convicted murder from harming someone who, for example, has been charge with painting graffiti on the side of a building). Fights still occur in each population of inmates. Tension is high because the prisoners have limited movement and must stay around one another for long stretches of time. Little things that might irritate a normal person often cause someone in jail to go into a rage. Any perceived slight can set off a fistfight. This can be so bad at times that some jails are referred to by their former inmates as "gladiator schools." Making it worse, when the officers rush in to break up such a fight, they often will use pepper spray or mace. In a closed-off area where vapors don't dissipate quickly, this leaves all inmates on the pod feeling as if they were the ones who have been sprayed.

In addition to the tension of daily life, jailhouse pods often provide little peace and quiet. Conversations grow loud as groups try to talk over one another. As inmates play games such as Spades, Hearts, or Poker, the loud slamming of cards onto steel picnic tables echoes off stone floors and cinderblock walls. Even at night when the inmates are locked in their cells, many still shout and carry on from behind the closed steel doors.

Before going any further, please note that the terms 'jail' and 'prison' are not interchangeable, though folks tend to use them that way. You might, for example, hear the anchorperson on the evening news say someone was "arrested and taken to prison" or that a judge sentenced someone to "forty years in jail." These are common mistakes.

Jail, as mentioned earlier, is a place used primarily for housing pretrial and misdemeanor inmates, or those convicted felons in transition between the courts and prisons. In the case of County Jails, these usually are run by the County Sheriff. In recent years, however, many areas across the country have switched to a Regional Jail system, where larger (sometimes privately-contracted) jails are built and managed by a Regional Jail Authority. Each Regional Jail usually houses inmates from several counties, with the cost of their incarceration paid for by the counties from which they come.

By contrast, prisons are long-term housing facilities for post-conviction felons. They have different levels of security—usually maximum, medium, and minimum—with the types of inmates held in each dependent upon their crimes, lengths of sentence, and how much time they have before parole eligibility or discharge. In the past, prisons were referred to as penitentiaries, as with the infamous Eastern State Penitentiary in Pennsylvania or the West Virginia Penitentiary at Moundsville. The term 'penitentiary' refers to the punitive nature of prisons. These days, most states rely more on rehabilitation, so the prisons have titles like Correctional Center or Correctional Facility. These are run by a state's Department of Corrections, and the cost of housing each inmate is paid by the state.

In addition to these, some states have classification facilities. These are somewhat of a cross between jails and prisons where a newly convicted felons will be taken, usually for a short time, while an assessment is made as to what level of incarceration that inmate will receive (maximum, medium, or minimum). There, the prisoners are measured with I.Q. tests and psychiatric evaluations, both of which can affect their classification.

Also, there are federal prisons which house those inmates convicted of federal crimes such as money laundering or racketeering, and ICE (Immigration and Customs Enforcement) facilities that house people facing immigration hearings and possible deportation.

Having read this, you might be picturing images from movies and television, seeing your loved one there and thinking how horrible that must be. Certainly, no one would want to spend time in any of these places. Even so, they are designed to hold all types of potential offenders, including those with anger-management and substance-abuse issues.

Now, let us take a look at what accommodations your loved one will have during the stay in jail. To begin with, there are three types of cells: 1) single occupancy, 2) double occupancy, and 3) dormitory style. Whether jail or prison, the single-occupancy cells are usually reserved for people in segregation (either administrative or punitive) and protective custody. In other words, they have violated institutional rules, are in personal danger, or have become a danger to others. The double-occupancy cell is the standard in most modern jails, although because of overcrowding, sometimes a third or fourth inmate will be moved into these. The dormitory-style cells house anywhere from four to forty inmates, and are much more common in prisons where movement is less controlled and inmates, because of their circumstances, are forced to interact with the same people for long periods of time.

In many modern jails, inside each cell will be stone or steel slabs protruding from the walls. On these will be placed thin, vinyl-coated foam mattresses similar to high-school wrestling mats. For shelving, there might be a metal ledge big enough to hold a small amount of paperwork, plus in some cases another stone or steel protrusion that serves as a crude desk or dining table. Also, on either the wall or ceiling, there will be a light that never shuts off. Some folks sarcastically refer to this as the "suicide light," because it allows a correctional officer to see inside the cell at any time and thus make sure everyone is still alive.

Inmates sometimes receive a Rubbermaid tub or vinyl carrying bag to store their clothes and commissary items. Jail clothing in most places consists of one- or two-piece cotton jumpsuits similar to the scrubs worn by nurses and orderlies.

The colors vary from state to state, although orange is the most common. Some jails use different colors to distinguish between men and women, or between felons, misdemeanants, and those awaiting trial. Most jails also have a separate color (probably yellow or neon green) set aside to distinguish inmates in segregation. Depending on how overcrowded the jail is at any given time, an inmate will receive anywhere from one to three of these jumpsuits. They also are given one to three pairs of underwear and socks, plus rubber flip-flops (shower shoes), that are worn continuously until the inmate can afford a cheap pair of sneakers from the commissary. Other clothing items that can be purchased from the commissary include gray sweatpants and plain, white t-shirts.

As for the clothing and other items worn or carried into the facility by someone under arrest, those are inventoried and stored until the person is released or transferred (if your loved one is later transferred, he or she might be permitted to transfer this property to you). Any cash not seized by the police will be added to a person's *inmate trustee account* (that is, money used for purchasing food, clothes, instant coffee, and other items such as stamps or playing cards, from the commissary), minus a set "booking" fee charged by most jails every time a person returns there from the streets. It is important to find out how much that booking fee is and keep it in mind when dropping off or sending money for an inmate. Should Ralph, for example, repeatedly be released on bond and have that bond revoked, the jail in most cases will charge him the booking fee each time he comes back. So, if Addie were to send Ralph fifty dollars to use for commissary, he might only receive a small portion of that the first time.

In many states, a fee also is taken out of the inmate trustee account for every *sick call*—the form that must be filled out to receive medical attention—visit to the medical unit, or new prescription ordered by the staff physician. These fees, ranging from two to five dollars, are the equivalent of the copay on most health-insurance plans. They can add up if an inmate repeatedly puts in sick calls, whether legitimate or otherwise. However, if a person has no money on his or her account, medical attention won't be denied. Instead, the inmate's account goes into a negative balance until the next time money is received.

It is important for anyone incarcerated to have at least some money available on the inmate trustee account, even if just enough for a candy bar and a bag of instant coffee every week. It also helps inmates to know a specific amount will be sent each month, however much that might be, so they know what they can spend at a given time.

Jail inmates also must purchase their own hygiene supplies such as shampoo and deodorant. While jails are required by law to provide some things such as soap and toilet paper, the other hygiene items a person might need just to feel like a human being are available from the commissary. The same is true for paper, writing implements, envelopes and stamps. Only if an inmate *never* receives money, will he or she be eligible for an indigent package, consisting of some hygiene products, a legal pad, and one or two stamped envelopes.

GRIEVANCES

Kendall was in jail awaiting trial. In a phone call to his mother, Jane, he told her he had been beaten. Now he said he had a black eye, and his glasses were broken. Jane called the jail's social worker to complain. When the social worker went to check on Kendall, he found the young man unmarked, getting ready to take a shower, and wearing his unbroken glasses.

Alvin told his father, Jack, that he had been triple-bunked in a two-man cell. Because of this, he had to sleep on the floor with his head near the steel toilet. When Jack called the jail, he was informed that no cell ever housed three inmates at a time.

Tyler, a Muslim, complained to his parents, Mitch and Michele, that he was being served pork hot dogs and sausage patties on his meal trays, in violation of his religious beliefs. When Mitch and Michele called to demand answers, they were informed that the meats were made from turkey rather than pork.

From time to time, issues will arise for inmates, some imagined or invented for the purpose of causing trouble, but others real and possibly serious. In every jail or prison, a grievance process has been established for filing a complaint against the institution. The grievance process will be different in different states and at different levels of incarceration, so it will be important for your inmate to read the jail's rulebook and learn those procedures.

Whatever the specific rules, the process will begin with the inmate filling out a grievance form which, if turned down, the inmate must then appeal to various levels. After the appeals, a case might be filed in outside court. In most cases, courts won't consider complaints until inmates have exhausted every possible avenue of the jail's grievance process. Why is that important? Without the ability to take the jail administrators to court, an inmate loses many remedies that might be available, including monetary ones.

Aside from the grievance process, if you suspect your loved one is having problems (things such as being beaten, triple-bunked in a two-man cell, served meal trays containing food not on his scheduled religious diet, and refused medical treatment or access to the law library), you might be able to resolve these by contacting the warden (or jail administrator), the social service department, or the jail's chaplain. Remember to be respectful during such a phone call. While all jail employees should act like professionals, it is still perfectly human to pass along maltreatment. Anger or contempt you show to a staff member might end up affecting your loved one and the treatment he receives.

SECURING AN INMATE'S RELEASE

Chas Smith was arrested for a serious charge that carried a long sentence. He claimed his innocence and begged his parents, Juan and Carla, to bail him out. The bond was set at $100,000, so the Smiths had to put their property up to cover it. Then, when Chas was released, he fled the area, causing his parents to lose their home.

As jail is such a hard place with such unpleasant conditions, you might wonder why inmates are left there for long periods of time. Ideally, they aren't. Those convicted of misdemeanors will be in jail for a short, fixed period of time, while felons will be transferred to prison as soon as possible. The main problem is with those awaiting trial on new charges. In most cases, bond will be set and, over time, lowered (as we will discuss in the next chapter) until a person can afford the cost. Because the county is paying for an inmate's incarceration before trial, county judges consider it best to make sure that almost every prisoner is released to wait out what might prove to be a lengthy trial process. Some impoverished misdemeanor inmates even end up being released on a Personal Recognizance bond, which means they sign a promise not to do anything stupid or commit crimes while out and, of course, to show up for their court hearings.

That said, there are several reasons why an inmate might not be released on bond. The judge, for example, might order that there be no bond set in the case for one of the following reasons: 1) the inmate faces a serious charge such as murder; 2) the inmate has failed to appear at court hearings in the past; 3) the inmate is from another state or county and, as such, more likely to flee; 4) the inmate has a hold or detainer placed on him from another jurisdiction (perhaps for an outstanding warrant in another state); or 5) the inmate has threatened the victim, witness, or other parties to the case; or 6) the inmate shows contempt for the judge during a hearing.

Sometimes substance abuse by the person plays a role. Judges often will wait a couple weeks before lowering a bond in order to make sure someone has detoxed from drugs and alcohol before release. Likewise, sometimes a condition of the bond will be drug treatment, and therefore an inmate will remain incarcerated until picked up by a staff member from an authorized drug and alcohol treatment facility.

Of course, the main reason an inmate stays in jail is that he or she doesn't have the resources to pay the bond. If a person has no money, and friends or family can't or won't come up with the funds, he or she will have to wait until the resolution of the case. Most families don't have large amounts of money. They might have some available, but not enough. If you find yourself in that situation, the best thing you can do is inform the defense lawyer how much you can afford. The lawyer then will discuss the case with the prosecutor and judge to get the bond lowered to that amount. In the end, the decision will be in the hands of the judge. While the judge usually accepts an agreement made between the prosecutor and the defense lawyer, doing so isn't mandatory.

Another option is a bail bondsman. Anyone who has ever seen one of the reality shows about bounty hunters will be familiar with bail bondsmen. They are the ones that hire bounty hunters in the event someone skips out on bond. An inmate will pay a non-refundable percentage (usually ten percent) of the actual bond, and the bondsman will assure the judge that the person, when released, will show up for all future court hearings. If the person doesn't show up, the bondsman will be on the hook for the entire bond. That's where the bounty hunters come in. If a client skips town, the bondsman will send a bounty hunter to locate and collect the person and bring him or her back for trial.

It sounds like a messy business. That's why not all states allow bail bondsmen to operate. The best way to find out if they are permitted to do business in your stare is to ask a lawyer or court clerk. Also, bail bondsmen usually have their information posted at jails and police stations where visitors can spot them easily.

VISITATION

If you plan to visit an inmate, whether in jail or prison, it is advisable that you call the facility first and find out its specific rules. Each institution will have different ways of doing things. All will have specific days and times set up during which a person may be visited. Some places require that you call and schedule a time for your visit, while others have visitation hours during which you show up and sign in. Some places allow contact visits, but others will involve a pane of shatterproof glass that separates you from your loved one. In a few places, video visitation is an option. Contact the institution to find out what the policies are.

While the visitation rules vary from jail to jail, there are many basic things common to most. Here are a few tips:

• *Bring two forms of identification, at least one with a picture of you.* In most places, these IDs will be scanned or photocopied and kept on file (however, you still must bring them every time). Each ID must be valid, so an expired driver's license, for example, might prevent you from visiting. This is necessary for several reasons. To begin with, there are people who will not be permitted to visit a particular inmate. Those people include the victim, the victim's family, and any witnesses for the state or charged coconspirators to the crime. The IDs also will be run through a national database to make sure there are no outstanding warrants for *your* arrest, and that you are allowed to be at the facility (many states have laws that ex-cons, for example, are not allowed to set foot on jailhouse or prison grounds after release).

• *Dress appropriately.* Again, different facilities have different standards for what is considered appropriate. Some places won't allow hats or hoodies. Mini-skirts and low-cut tops or anything else that exposes too much of the body often aren't allowed. A common reason for turning away a visitor is underwire in a brassiere. Your best bet is to call ahead of time and find out what might keep you from seeing your loved one.

• *You will go through a metal detector, so keep jewelry to a minimum.* In fact, many places won't permit jewelry at all. The same is true with purses, wallets, and electronics. Often, visitors are asked to leave these in their vehicles, or else they are given a locker in which to store them during their visit.

• *Never try to take items into a visit that would be considered contraband inside the jail or prison.* Never take alcohol or tobacco. No drugs are allowed, whether illegal or prescription. No weapons will be permitted, including such minor items as pocket knives or nail files. Phones, too, aren't allowed in most jails.

• *There are other reasons for which you might be refused.* For example, you are not on the visiting list or were recently incarcerated in the same facility.

• *Cameras observe almost everything.* Needless to say, you should be on your best behavior.

• *Visits may be canceled at any time.* In most cases, you won't be given a reason. It might be something you or the inmate did, but it also could be a security drill, a fire in the kitchen, or a medical emergency that will cause the jail to be locked down while outside EMS personnel are brought in to deal with the crisis. If you are told the visit has been canceled, stay calm and exit as instructed.

• *If your vehicle is parked on jail or prison grounds, it can be checked for drugs or weapons without a search warrant.*

Bringing even a licensed weapon onto jailhouse grounds is a crime.

• *If you cause a disturbance or break the rules, you might not be permitted back in the future.* In fact, it is likely that you won't be allowed to visit your loved one again. Remember, they have your IDs on file.

PHONE CALLS

Perry called his 18-year-old girlfriend, Lilly, every day from jail. He convinced her that listening to music over the telephone helped him relax. So, when he called, she held the phone up to the radio for almost the full fifteen minutes. Then, Perry would hang up the phone and call right back. He did this several times a day. When Lilly's parents received their telephone bill, they were shocked to see it was several hundred dollars.

One of the problems related to jail is the telephone. You, even as a family member, can't call an inmate. The incarcerated person must initiate the call. Even then, the phones may be used only at certain times. If they are in the cell itself, the phones often will be turned off at night and back on in the morning, as well as at other scheduled times (commissary call, shift change, etc.). If the telephones are in the pod area, the prisoners have no access to them at night and during other times when they are locked in their cells. Furthermore, telephones in the pod area must be shared by all inmates living in that pod. So, finding the phone free long enough for an inmate to make a call is not always easy.

The biggest problem for most people is the cost. Institutions have arrangements with specific telephone companies to run the phone systems. Both the company and the jail make a profit from this. All calls come with charges reversed. Most have an initial fee of several dollars, followed by a per-minute rate. This can be expensive. In addition, while the maximum duration of a call usually is limited to ten or fifteen minutes, nothing prevents the inmate from hanging up and calling back right away if no one else is waiting for the phone.

Aside from the cost, you should keep in mind that *your* phone company might not allow collect calls or calls from jails and prisons. This is especially true of some of the internet companies that promise cheaper rates. Certain devices such as those designed to block "robo-calls" also will prevent your loved one from getting through to you.

There are two ways these issues might be resolved. First, if you contact the company that handles the phone system (this number should be taped to the phone where it easily can be located), you will be able to set up a prepaid account. You only receive calls while money is on account, allowing you to set limits as to how much you are willing to spend each month. If the money runs out, the calls stop until more money is added. Second, many institutions sell phone cards from the commissary, with limits on the number of cards than can be purchased each week. If your friend or family member has funds available on the inmate trustee account, these cards can be purchased and used for direct dialing.

Another important thing to remember about telephone use is that calls are recorded and monitored, excluding those between an inmate and his or her lawyer. Be careful what you talk about or allow your loved one to say. Information regarding the criminal case can be used against the inmate at trial. Also, any threats the inmate might make against people on the outside will be recorded and can affect bond hearings or sentencing, and they might result in additional criminal charges. In addition, if your loved one is despondent while talking on the phone and threatens to commit suicide, one of officers assigned to listen to calls likely will have heard and reported it (even so, when you hang up, call the facility and let administration know, just in case the person wasn't overheard). That will result in his or her being taken to a holding cell, stripped, and observed until a staff psychiatrist is convinced that the danger has passed.

Use of the telephone can be a positive and beneficial thing for an inmate. However, there are other means of communication. Cards and letters also are a good way to show your loved one that you care. They allow for longer, more extensive messages, and invite the inmate to write you back. Anyone stuck behind bars has nothing but time, and writing letters is a good way to pass that time. Again, keep in mind that the mail can and often will be read by jail employees. If you send five letters, it is a safe bet that all five will be opened and examined for contraband, and at least two will be read.

EMERGENCIES AND FURLOUGHS

Toby, a young man in his teens, reported to the chaplain that his infant son had died. Toby asked the chaplain to file the paperwork for a furlough so that Toby might attend the funeral. The chaplain passed the case along to the jail's social worker who, in turn, sought information about the deceased child by contacting several funeral homes in the area, the coroner's office in all surrounding counties, and finally the family. It turned out that Toby didn't have a child. Nonetheless, he thanked the chaplain and social worker for their help in his time of grief. Both were unsure if Toby suffered from a mental illness or merely wanted a way out of jail.

If there is a family emergency such as the death of a close relative, the best way to contact the inmate is to call the jail and ask for the watch commander (also called the shift commander). This is the person in charge of the staff and officers during any given period of the day. The watch commander will ensure that your loved one gets the message.

In such a situation, your inmate might need spiritual guidance from the jail's chaplain or counseling from the social worker. Your loved one should not be afraid to ask for help.

If the emergency does involve the death of a close family member, a furlough might be requested as in Toby's case above. Different states have different rules for furloughs. Some don't allow them at all. If your state does, there will be forms to fill out. This is most often handled by either the chaplain, the social worker, or the defense lawyer. Those forms will work their through the system to the judge overseeing a person's case. The judge then decides whether an inmate will be released or escorted to attend a funeral. The judge can deny the request, grant a furlough, or lower the inmate's bond for immediate release.

Should a person be granted a furlough, remember to get him or her back to the jail on time. Failure to return on time is considered an escape, could result in additional charges, and will affect every aspect of your loved one's case from bond hearings and work release to his eventual eligibility for parole.

TIPS

Now you have a good idea of what jail is like and how to deal with issues that arise. The following are a few additional things to remember as your loved one's case moves forward:

• *This is a long process.* You have time to make decisions, so don't panic.

• *The responsibility for all of this is the inmate's not yours.* Do what you can when you can. There's no need to cause yourself more stress than you already feel.

• *If it's the inmate's money, he or she decides; if it's your money, you decide.* Don't overspend without considering the consequences for you and your future. At the same time, you shouldn't hold back your loved one's money without a good reason.

• *It takes weeks, sometimes months, for a person to think clearly after detoxing from drugs or alcohol.* Your loved one will come around in time, at which point the two of you might start to understand each other better.

• *Your inmate's lawyer will only interact with you when there are changes in the case.* Each case will have long stretches of inaction, so be patient. Remember, everything goes slowly in the system.

• *Incarcerated people might say or do anything to get out.*

• *You are hearing only one side of the story.* This is true when a lawyer speaks in court, but also when you talk to your loved one on the phone.

• *An inmate does have rights.* Get help if you believe those rights are being violated.

• *All institutional rules are there for a reason.* This is true even when they seem unreasonable. They are not aimed at you, so try not to let them upset you.

• *This is a stressful situation.* You already know that. Now find someone with whom you can talk about and share your frustrations. Nothing good will come from holding your feelings inside.

Part II.
In the Courts

HENRY'S CASE

HENRY WAS A SLIM FELLOW in his mid-twenties. Clean-cut and mild-mannered, he always kept his head down and made no real impression on the people he passed on the streets. No one who knew him expected what came next.

Henry was arrested and charged with murder for what the newspapers described as the "vicious" killing of an elderly woman. He was taken to the county jail, booked into the system, and held without bond because of the seriousness of the crime. If convicted, he would be eligible for the death penalty. Henry remained locked up for a long time while his case worked its way through the courts.

While awaiting his trial, Henry kept to himself, rarely communicating with the staff or other inmates. The jail's educators, however, tried to get to know him, and they discovered that he struggled with learning difficulties. He had a speech problem also, because of which he talked as little as possible.

Henry had only one visitor, a brother, during this time. It turned out that he had little contact with his parents and other siblings. They led an isolated life in a rural setting. They cared about Henry but didn't know how to help him. Though they didn't say it, they also might have been afraid because of the nature of the crime Henry allegedly committed.

Because Henry's family members had not been in contact, the educators were unable to prepare them for what to expect. Henry's lawyer would have been the logical choice to inform them, but that young public defender was dealing with his first death-penalty case. Such cases were rare in the area, and the lawyer was too busy figuring out his strategy to explain things to Henry's family.

After several months of delays and a lengthy trial, Henry was convicted of first-degree murder with special circumstances (the brutality of the crime), which made him eligible for capital punishment. He stood, head bowed, before the judge and listened as he was sentenced to die by lethal injection. As required by state law, an execution date was scheduled for a date less than three months away.

Loud gasps were heard coming from the family. Neither Henry nor his family members expected this to happen. They also didn't realize that there were automatic appeals or that most death-penalty cases would go on for ten years or more before an execution occurred. It was only after they left the courtroom that someone explained the process and assured Henry's parents and siblings that many other legal steps would be taken and, if those were lost, still many years would pass before Henry would be executed.

Neither the jury in convicting Henry nor the judge in sentencing him had considered the young man's mental state. The lawyer failed to put on evidence that Henry wasn't taking his required, necessary psychiatric medications on the night the crime occurred. Also that night, as Henry later admitted, he ingested a mind-altering drug for the first time.

After spending two years on death row, the judge ordered that Henry be brought back to the courthouse for a reconsideration-of-sentence hearing. All Henry's mental issues were brought to light. Because of that, the prosecutor, at the judge's urging, offered Henry a deal. Henry would be resentenced to life in prison without the possibility of parole.

Henry's story reminds us that few of us are aware of the intricacies of the legal system. Most things that occur are written in the law. Judges, prosecutors, and defense lawyers must follow the law. That is why it is so important to have good legal representation and advice. The more you know and understand what happens in the legal system, the better off you will be as you and your loved ones work your way through it.

INTRODUCTION TO THE LEGAL SYSTEM

The Legal system in the United States can be complicated. There are many jurisdictions that overlap almost like concentric circles. The federal government passes its laws which are dealt with by the federal courts. However, there also are laws and regulations passed by each state, county and city or municipality, all of which are dealt with in local courts by various judges and magistrates. The laws themselves are often modified by the Congress (federal), state legislatures, city councils and so on. As if that weren't confusing enough, legislators often model their laws after laws from other states, so there might be similarities among various states. However, there can be extreme differences as well. Consider Henry's case, for example. Had Henry been tried in Massachusetts, the death penalty never would have been an option because that state does not allow for it. In Texas, on the other hand, the death penalty would be considered almost every time.

All laws, regardless of what legislative body passes them, must comply with the dictates of the Constitution of the United States, and many laws eventually get struck down because they fail in this regard. Testing the Constitutionality of a law is done after losing a case (with rare exceptions) and appealing along the chain of federal courts: District Courts, Courts of Appeals, and the Supreme Court of the United States—the ultimate arbiter. Also, if a person has a federal case or is charged with a federal crime, then federal laws take precedence (that is, they go first). At the same time, there are offenses such as bank robbery and kidnapping for a which a person can be charged, tried and convicted in both federal *and* state courts.

Needless to say, it is important to gather as much information as you can, both about the laws in question and the courts in which a case will be tried.

Now that you've had a brief look at the confusing, often interconnected court system, here are a few things to keep in mind as you see the process through:

• *TV is not reality.* Only on television will cases come to trial and reach a resolution quickly. There will be no austere Perry Mason hammering a witness until he confesses. Nor is it guaranteed that the evidence for innocence or guilt will be so convincing that reasonable people won't disagree as to what the outcome should be. Television court shows give a false sense of what being in court is like. Real cases tend to move slowly, with hearing after hearing taking place before anything resembling a trial occurs. Many things can cause delays. For example, a mental health evaluation of an inmate might be necessary for determining if he or she is competent to stand trial. Tests on evidence such as blood, hair, fibers, and DNA can take a long time because of backlogs in the processing facilities. Some courts also have backlogs.

• *Emotional involvement clouds judgment.* This is why

rational people, even qualified lawyers, need other lawyers to represent them. As Abraham Lincoln famously said, "He who represents himself has a fool for a client." When you have a personal stake in a case, whether you face your own trial or that of a friend or loved one, you won't see all the issues clearly. It might seem to you like the entire system is set up to convict the defendant, whatever the crime. After all, the prosecutor has seemingly unlimited resources. In reality though, many of the steps and even delays in the process are meant to insure that the rights of the defendant are respected. Often you will be better off if you relax and allow the defense attorney — who sees the situation more clearly and objectively — to do whatever needs to be done.

• *The system is fair but has pitfalls.* Some court officials are elected, and therefore part of the political system. Sheriffs, states' attorneys (prosecutors), and circuit clerks gain their offices by popular vote on Election Day. Federal judges are appointed to their positions, but in many states, the local judges are elected to theirs. This can impact cases where the publicity involved might directly affect the next election. "Tough on crime" is a phrase heard often in political campaigns. Thus a prosecutor will strive for a maximum punishment to improve his or her appearance of inflexibility. Judges, though ethically bound to be fair and unbiased, nonetheless might give out harsher sentences as November draws near. Because of this, some lawyers will use delaying strategies to postpone trials or sentencings in high-profile cases until after election time in hope of eliminating politics as a factor.

• *The public and news media will be in the courtroom.* Court cases and most hearings, excluding those involving juveniles, are required to be open to the public in order to ensure fairness. This might be uncomfortable for you. Moreover, in high-profile cases, the crowds of press and onlookers might be so large that special arrangements must to be made to determine which folks will get to watch. Those present are expected to be dressed appropriately, to be silent, and not cause any form of distraction. This includes muting ringers on cell phones, not taking photos, and refraining from outbursts. The bailiff, often a deputy sheriff specifically assigned to the court, keeps order and will remove anyone whose behavior is inappropriate.

• *If you are listed as a witness, whether for the defense or prosecution, you might be excluded from the courtroom.* This is to ensure that your testimony will not be affected by hearing the testimony of others whose accounts may vary from yours. If you have questions about the case or what might be required of you, ask the lawyer—the attorney for the defense, unless you are testifying for the prosecution. If you have questions about the procedure or scheduling, ask the bailiff who either can answer your questions or will direct you to the person that can.

• *Not everything said on TV or in the newspapers is true.* If you are not present in the courtroom, you might feel the urge to find out what you missed by watching the news or reading the next day's morning paper. Sometimes this can hurt more than help. Reporters are human and make errors. Even when they get the facts right, reporters and commentators will miss some details that might be important, or else take statements out of context. A reporter's choice of what to include or exclude in a story will affect how readers or viewers see the case. After many hours of testimony each day, only a brief summary can be reported, and each writer will have a different take on that day's events. In fact, there have been times when competing newspapers in the same city have reported two entirely different versions of what happened in a case. This has proven especially true in larger cities such as New York and Los Angeles where there might be multiple newspapers, all with different editorial boards, sales figures, and target audiences.

WHO'S WHO

Next, it will be important for you to familiarize yourself with the people you are likely to see in a courtroom. Each will have a part to play in what, at times, might seem like a theatrical production. They are as follows:

• *The judge.* This person presides over the case, listens to legal arguments, makes rulings of law, sets the dates for hearings and trials, sets bail for a defendant, and issues sentencing orders in the event of a guilty plea or verdict. Several judges will preside over different parts of a case, though this varies from state to state and, sometimes, from jurisdiction to jurisdiction. The magistrate, for example, often presides over initial appearances and preliminary hearings in felony cases, and over the entire process for misdemeanors. In the event the magistrate finds probable cause for a felony charge, the case will then be bound over to a higher ranking judge, one usually with a title such as Circuit Judge or Superior Court Judge. In federal court, cases go before the District Judge. Whatever their titles, judges are referred to directly as, "Your Honor," and in written documents as "The Honorable Judge _____."

In the courtroom, the judge has total responsibility for the operation of the court. As such, the judge informs the defendant of his or her rights, reads the charges, listens to arguments by the lawyers, makes decisions on all motions, gives formal legal instructions required by law (including those to the jury), confirms the jury's decision after one has been made, and orders the sentence after a guilty verdict or plea. The judge also will listen to and observe everything said on the witness stand, sometimes asking questions directly (though this is limited in most cases).

Though the judge runs the courtroom based on each state's Rules of Criminal Procedure and Rules of Evidence, personality still impacts how this is handled. Judges over time will develop a reputation for being defense- or prosecution-minded (though these might prove to be myths more than facts). Some judges are referred to as "hang'em" judges, a reference to times long ago when major crimes were punished by a swift hanging in the public square. Even so, remember that you can't choose which judge will oversee your loved one's case. Judges are assigned to their cases and won't easily give them up. That said, if there is a good reason for a judge to be removed, the defense attorney might file a motion for recusal. For the lawyer to succeed, the reasons behind the motion must be extreme. It would be unfair to the defendant, for example, if the judge were related to one of the victims or had been a victim of the defendant in a previous crime.

In a high-profile case, the defense also might request a change of venue. That is, the defense will ask that the case be moved to another jurisdiction because the local publicity "poisoned the pool of potential jurors," making it impossible for the defendant to receive a fair trial. This happened in the trial of Timothy McVeigh, who detonated the truck bomb in front of the Alfred P. Murrah Federal Building in Oklahoma City, Oklahoma, killing many. The case was to be tried in federal court in Oklahoma City, but at the request of the defense, was moved to Denver, Colorado. Keep in mind, however, that this doesn't necessarily rid the defendant of a particular judge. The judge might travel with the case.

• *The state's attorney (also, district attorney or prosecutor).* This is the lawyer that represents "the people" or "the state," as well as "the victim." In smaller jurisdictions, the state's attorney handles all cases. In larger jurisdictions, however, the elected prosecutor will oversee the distribution of cases to various employees known as assistant prosecutors.

The role of the state's attorney is to prosecute the case. He or she does this by seeking an indictment, filing motions, responding to defense motions, presenting evidence, questioning and cross-examining witnesses, etc. The prosecutor must prove the defendant guilty of the crime "beyond a reasonable doubt." At the same time, however, a prosecutor has the ethical responsibility to seek "the best interests of justice." That allows for plea-bargaining, but also means that when evidence arises that shows a defendant is innocent, the prosecutor should request that all relevant charges be dropped.

• *The defense attorney.* This lawyer represents the defendant. The role of the defense attorney is to provide information and advice to the defendant, make legal arguments, file motions (to exclude certain evidence, for example), and do everything possible to ensure the defendant has a fair trial, regardless of innocence or guilt. Of course, a not-guilty verdict will not always be possible, so the defense attorney also must engage in plea-deal negotiations with the prosecutor.

There are two types of defense attorneys. First, there are paid lawyers that will charge an amount of money depending on the type of case, how much time will be involved, and their own personal reputations. You (or the defendant) must give them a retainer (an amount of money), sometimes rather large, that acts as a down payment for their services. Depending on the type of case, some paid lawyers might negotiate a set fee to cover everything up until a verdict is reached (appeals always cost extra). A paid lawyer will accept reversed-charge telephone calls from incarcerated clients. They will meet with their clients on a regular basis and keep them informed of any changes in the case. Some of these lawyers are specialists in criminal law, but others handle many types of cases, including lawsuits, divorces, wills, estates, etc. They might work in different jurisdictions if needed, though for different states, they often will need to hire other lawyers licensed to practice in those states. Most paid lawyers are honest and will provide good services for their fees. They have a local reputation to maintain, and they will do the best they can for you or your loved one. Your best bet is to hire the most well-respected lawyer that can you afford.

If, however, the defendant can't afford a lawyer, even with your financial help, he or she still is entitled to representation. The judge will appoint the second type of lawyer, the public defender, to represent your loved one. The public defender is a lawyer paid by the state for just that purpose. There often will be several of them working out of the same office. Public defenders are assigned. *You don't get to choose the lawyer you want.*

Public defenders can be quite good at their jobs because of the number of clients they handle. After working many criminal cases, they get to know the judges and prosecutors. They learn from practical experience what will and won't work. They become familiar with the members of local law enforcement. They will use all this knowledge for your loved one's benefit.

These lawyers, unfortunately, are often overwhelmed with cases, sometimes handling seventy to a hundred cases at a time. They will work as hard as they can for your loved one, but don't have the same time and resources to devote to each case that a paid lawyer does. As such, they likely will have little contact with their clients and, when they do get in touch, it tends to be by mail. Collect calls from jail aren't accepted unless there are special circumstances, and these usually are planned in advance. The best attribute of public defenders, however, is that because of their excessive caseload, they become skilled negotiators when the time comes for plea-bargaining. They will get your loved one the best deal available.

There is one other thing to note about public defenders: not all of their expenses are automatically covered by the state. To pay for expert witnesses or unusual tests on evidence, these lawyers must seek permission from the judge. The judge, in most cases, will allow the public defender to do what is needed, but it isn't guaranteed. Furthermore, some states allow the judge to add up all costs, including the fees paid by the state to the public defender, and charge them to the defendant in any eventual restitution order. In other words, if your loved one pleads guilty or is convicted of a crime, part of his or her sentence might include paying the lawyer's fees and expenses.

• *Others with a role to play.* There are other employees you likely will see in a courtroom. These include the court reporter (a stenographer who takes down everything said during hearings and trials and transcribes the official record); the bailiff (often a deputy sheriff or retired police officer who keeps order in the courtroom, announces the judge, observes the proceedings, and prevents distractions); and the court clerks (who keep records and schedules, handle court files, follow the judge's instructions to facilitate the court's functions).

• *Jailhouse Lawyers.* You will not see these people in the courtroom as they are prisoners themselves, but they might have an influence (whether positive or negative) on your loved one. Jailhouse lawyers are inmates trained to assist in the jail's law library. 'Trained,' though, can have different meanings. While these sometimes might be actual lawyers who have been arrested, they also might be self-taught. Some inmates will spend a great of time in the law library, either studying up on their own cases or reading law books. They often will do legal work for other inmates, including writing briefs or motions, filing lawsuits, or just generally discussing the facts and laws of a case. These people are not real lawyers, however, and the things they say or do for your loved one should be checked by the defense attorney. In addition, your loved one should be careful in dealing with jailhouse lawyers. They often have different motives for doing legal work. Some want commissary or favors as payment. Others just want to show off how much they know. A few might even be "snitches," trying to learn information about your loved one's case that might be traded to the prosecutor for a better plea bargain.

PLEA DEALS

In the majority of cases, the defense lawyer and the prosecutor or assistant prosecutor will get together and work out a plea deal that is in the best interests of both the state and the defendant. In such cases, the defendant benefits by receiving a lesser sentence and possibly a lesser charge or reduction in the number of charges, while the state benefits by getting a conviction without having to spend the time and money required to take a case to trial. In Henry's case above, for example, the eventual plea deal allowed Henry to avoid the death penalty, while the prosecutor nonetheless ensured that Henry would be punished by spending the rest of his life in prison.

Aside from financial and time considerations, the state's attorney might offer the defendant a plea deal for the sake of the victim or victim's family in a case. This is true especially in sexual assault cases, where sparing the victim further humiliation and intimidation is a benefit that must be factored into any decision. Also, it is a common tactic in child sexual abuse cases where the psychological well-being of the abused child is a concern.

Another thing to consider is that prosecutors sometimes offer better deals to defendants willing to cooperate with law enforcement for the purpose of capturing other criminals. This also happens when one defendant agrees to testify against other defendants, whether in the same case or a different one.

Whatever the circumstances, the defense attorney will negotiate the best deal possible. Even so, the defendant must choose whether to accept it. No plea deal can be forced upon a defendant.

Once the defendant accepts a plea deal, it goes to the judge for approval. A judge, however, is not bound by any deal the prosecutor makes. Most of the time, the judge will agree, but if the "interests of justice" are not met by the deal, then the plea bargain will be thrown out.

ADDITIONAL NOTES ABOUT LAWYERS

• *The public defender's office also has investigators, paralegals, and secreteries.* The secretary for any lawyer is a key person to get to know. Often the lawyers and paralegals will be busy or in court, so the secretary will take your call, making sure the lawyer gets a written message which will be placed in the defendant's file.

• *Sometimes it helps if the lawyer is local.* This isn't always true. In larger cities, it makes no difference at all. However, in a small, close-knit community, a well-liked Atticus Finch-type lawyer can accomplish things that strangers might not.

• *A person can act as his or her own lawyer.* This is referred to as *pro se*, meaning for him/herself. For reasons discussed earlier, this isn't advisable. When lawyers and judges get in trouble, even they hire other lawyers.

• *The lawyers who advertise on TV and promise they will only get paid if they win do not handle criminal cases.* These are civil lawyers that deal with lawsuits, usually involving personal injury. They take cases in which they expect to win money, and then are paid about a third of whatever funds are received at the end of a case. It is considered unethical for a lawyer to offer such a deal in a criminal case, and any lawyer doing so would risk being disbarred.

• **Under some circumstances, a paid lawyer will take a case pro bono** *(free of charge).* This is rare, however, so you shouldn't expect it.

OTHER ISSUES

Before we proceed into the courtroom for a look at the various steps in the process, it is important that we stop to take a look at a couple of issues that might arise, depending on a defendant's situation. The following are the stories of Sally and Ivan. They are extreme opposites. In Sally's case, she has no friends or family in the courtroom. In Ivan's case, Ivan's family is there but might prefer not to be. These are examples of what might happen.

ALONE: SALLY'S CASE

Sally was a pleasant young woman, mild of temperament, with a soft, southern drawl. She seemed polite and well educated. However, she was alone. She had no visitors, received no mail, and had no commissary funds during her entire stay in jail. Not much was known about her. She gave a name that might have been an alias, though no one could be certain because she had no identification and a database search using her fingerprints turned up no prior record.

In this case, Sally had been accused of fraud related to a check-cashing scheme. Her friend, who had been arrested with her, posted bond and was released, disappearing and leaving Sally to face the court alone.

The prosecutor offered Sally a deal. He wanted her to provide information about other people connected to the crime.

Sally chose to remain silent.

When the time came for her to go to court, she asked for a bench trial and was found guilty by the judge. He sentenced her to time served plus two years of unsupervised probation. Sally faced the proceedings bravely. She listened carefully and responded with dignity.

Sally was religious and, when she left the jail, she went to a church mission in a big city. She said she planned to start again.

It is hard to stand in the courtroom and face a judge, even in the best circumstances. Now imagine how much harder it must be to deal with such traumatic events alone. For most defendants, it will prove helpful to have family and friends there to offer support.

That doesn't mean that you, as a family member, must quit your job and spend every waking minute at the courthouse. The defendant will understand if you can't be there for all hearings. Even if you miss half a dozen minor hearings, however, being there for the trial and the sentencing are important. Those are the times your loved one will need the most support. In addition, your presence will show the judge that the defendant has friends and relatives that care. In cases involving crimes considered less serious, this might sway the judge as to whether to sentence a person to prison or some alternative punishment like home confinement or probation.

Even if the judge and jury are unaware of your presence, your loved one will know. Having family there often serves as a crutch to help a person face this difficult process.

AN UGLY CRIME: IVAN'S CASE

Ivan was arrested and accused of molesting a child. The police had gathered a significant amount of physical evidence, which included DNA samples taken from the victim, tested, and found to be a match with Ivan's DNA. A family member caught Ivan in a compromising situation with the child. When questioned by a social worker, the child identified Ivan and offered a detailed description of what had happened.

The prosecutor offered Ivan a deal in which Ivan would plead guilty to a lesser charge, serve several years in prison, and then register for the rest of his life as a sex offender. The prosecutor explained that if this case went to trial, the child would have to testify, which would be a bad thing for everyone involved. In that event, the prosecutor assured Ivan that he would ask for the maximum possible sentence.

Ivan refused to admit he did anything inappropriate. The public defender, the social worker, and the jail's chaplain each explained to Ivan the seriousness of the charges against him. All encouraged him to plead guilty and accept the shorter sentence, but Ivan wouldn't agree. Perhaps he couldn't face up to what he had done as though he had blocked it from him his mind so that it seemed as though it never really happened. It was also possible that he suffered from a mental illness that kept him from remembering or processing those events. Whatever the case, Ivan remained adamant about his innocence.

Many family members showed up for his trial. They sat through the child's vivid, ugly testimony. They saw evidence presented that made them physically and emotionally ill. They listened carefully as the prosecutor attacked Ivan's character and made him out to be a monster.

Ivan was convicted and, as expected, the judge sentenced him to

the maximum term in prison. Older and in poor health, Ivan likely
would die there.

It can be extremely difficult for family members to
listen to what is being said in court about a close friend or
family member. In general, the only things that come up
are negative. A defendant might be the nicest woman in the
world, but the prosecutor will stand up say *she's a flight risk,*
a danger to the community, a known drug addict. Likewise, a
man might never have had so much as a traffic ticket, yet the
judge, during sentencing, will speak down to him as if he is
the most horrible man that ever lived. These things will shock
you and upset you. If you believe your loved one is innocent,
they will seem like slander. You will feel angry, sad, shocked,
and more than a little helpless. Even if you know your loved
one is guilty, it might seem impossible to listen without an
emotional reaction because you know the good side of the
person.

Details of a violent case are especially shocking and
offensive. You might hear things you know are not true,
although there might be photographs or scientific evidence
that seem straightforward. The best thing you can do in these
situations is to take notes about questionable statements,
dates, and other information sounding inaccurate or blatantly
false to you. Share these notes with the defense attorney.

However, try not to upset yourself if the lawyer chooses
not to use the information you provide. A lawyer's defense
strategy can be complicated and often requires leaving
seemingly important things unsaid. The defense attorney
knows what information the prosecutor has, and it may be in
the defendant's best interest to keep certain facts concealed.

They might be brought up at a later time, or they might be left out of the case entirely. Either way, the defense attorney has a strategy and will go forward with it.

Your loved one might complain to you about the lawyer's actions or seeming inaction. What the defendant says could be accurate, but it also might not be. Sometimes defendants are so concerned with minor issues that they fail to see the larger picture. Of course, while in jail, a person has nothing but time to spend thinking about every little detail of a case.

Don't dismiss your loved one's claims, but also try to stay calm. Consult with the defense attorney, but remember that getting angry and yelling at the lawyer won't help anyone.

Lastly, if your loved one is facing an ugly charge like Ivan's or one involving some other crime of violence, there will be evidence—testimony, photographs, videos, etc.—that you might find offensive and disturbing to see. If you anticipate something of that nature, you might choose not to be in the courtroom on that day. Sometimes the judge will order a recess before particularly unpleasant evidence is presented. If that happens, you can leave the courtroom and wait outside until the next break. How much of the trial you see is up to you.

TYPES OF HEARINGS PRIOR TO TRIAL

If you have watched any of the courtroom procedural shows on television, you might be under the impression that criminal cases go straight from the interrogation to the courthouse for trial. That isn't reality, however. Your loved one will go through many steps in the court process before seeing a trial.

In fact, the majority of cases never make it that far. Most end in a guilty plea to one charge or another. Some are dismissed by the judge in response to motions by the defense attorney. Other cases are withdrawn by the prosecutor if it becomes clear that there is not enough evidence for a conviction. Still, for those people who do take their cases all the way to a trial, there are several types of hearings to go through first.

We will take a look at those now.

• *Initial Appearance.* This will be a person's first time in front of a judge. Usually a magistrate will handle these, and in most jurisdictions one will be on duty and assigned to oversee all initial appearances on a given day. The initial appearance is sometimes referred to as an arraignment and often will have many of the same features, such as the reading of charges, the entering of a plea, and the setting of bond. All defendants in all jurisdictions are entitled to an initial appearance of one form or another *within a reasonable amount of time.* It serves two functions: 1) to make sure the defendant is aware of his rights (to remain silent, to speak to an attorney, etc.), and 2) to protect the defendant from statements made during coercive interrogations (which can include everything from threats of physical violence by the police officers to their simply continuing to question a person after he or she has asked for an attorney).

The time frame in which an initial appearance takes place is critical. Often, it will be on the same day as the arrest. However, what is considered a reasonable amount of time varies. Some jurisdictions allow the defendant to be held in jail for a little longer. Regardless of what amount of time is accepted as reasonable, if the magistrate deems that the defendant was held beyond that time before an initial appearance, sanctions will be levied against the state in that all confessions and evidence gathered in the interval will be thrown out. With minor crimes, sometimes the entire case will be dismissed.

Another function of the initial appearance is to establish probable cause for holding the defendant. This is true especially if an arrest was made without an arrest warrant. Even so, the standard for probable cause at an initial appearance is rather low. Usually the police reports are enough, and no other evidence will be presented.

One thing to keep in mind about the initial appearance is that you, in all likelihood, won't be there. In fact, often there will be no prosecutors or defense attorneys either. In many jurisdictions, to save the time and effort of transporting a defendant to court, the initial appearance will be conducted by video conference with the magistrate (sometimes even in the early a.m. hours). Don't be concerned. If your loved one doesn't have a lawyer yet, the magistrate will enter a not-guilty plea and refer the case to the public defender's office.

In some jurisdictions, you might hear the initial appearance referred to as a "bond hearing." In almost all instances, bond will be set (or denied, if the case is extreme). The size of the bond depends on a number of factors: the nature of the crime, the defendant's criminal record, whether the defendant has a history of escape or failing to show up for court appearances, whether the defendant is homeless, what is in the best interests of public safety (if the defendant has made threats against the victim, for example), etc. The more serious the charge, the higher the initial bond will be. If a person is drunk or high on drugs, bond also might be set at a higher level as a way of forcing the defendant to detox before release. Furthermore, should a defendant anger the magistrate, bond might be higher or denied altogether until proper respect is shown.

Remember, court cases take a long time, the county benefits by having a defendant make bond and await trial at home. That relieves jail overcrowding and defers the cost of housing to the individual. It should be noted, however, that for these same reasons, a defendant who fails to make bond might receive a faster trial. A case is much more likely to be delayed for long periods of time while a defendant is out on bond.

Many jurisdictions consider home confinement or drug rehab as conditions of issuing bond in felony cases. These cost the defendant money, but are considered beneficial to the public. If these are an option for your loved one, they should be fully considered because days spent on home confinement or in drug rehab often will be added to the "time served" during the sentencing phase after a conviction.

• *Preliminary Hearing.* The next time the defendant goes before a judge, it will be for a preliminary hearing. This is a mini-trial meant for determining if there is probable cause to bind the case over to the Grand Jury. The magistrate might hear this, or it might have already been kicked over to a felony (Circuit, Superior, etc.) court.

These hearings are tricky because the prosecutor must put on actual evidence, question witnesses, and make arguments, but the result almost always will be a finding of probable cause. In other words, it requires a lot of effort for little gain. As such, this can be a place in the process where deals are made, mainly in regard to reducing a defendant's bond. The prosecutor frequently will agree to a lower bond if the defense attorney agrees to waive the preliminary hearing. It serves as a win for both parties.

• **Bond Reduction Hearing.** For the most part, prior to an indictment, the defendant will return to court only after a motion is made by one of the lawyers. The most common of these hearings is the bond reduction hearing. The judge might order the defendant brought back to court several times, possibly lowering the bond on each occasion. These hearings happen on short notice, however, so be prepared to drop everything and hurry to court. The presence of a defendant's friends and family can reassure the judge when ruling on lowering bond.

• **Grand Jury Hearing.** The Grand Jury is a panel of citizens chosen from the county in which charges have been brought. Once a case is bound over to the Grand Jury, a closed hearing takes place during which the prosecutor presents evidence and the testimony of witnesses. In almost every case, neither the defendant nor defense attorney will be present. The Grand Jury listens to all evidence and then will issue an *indictment*, which is a formal charge based on the laws and statutes of the state. It must be quite specific as to the allegations. If a defendant faces multiple charges, some might be dismissed during this process. Others can be reduced to lesser charges (manslaughter instead of murder, for example). The Grand Jury makes its decision based strictly on what evidence the prosecutor presents. However, don't expect all charges against your loved one to be thrown out. This rarely happens. In fact, a common phrase repeated in law schools is that a prosecutor can get the Grand Jury to indict a ham sandwich if he chooses.

Some states allow the defense attorney to waive the Grand Jury process as well. If this happens, the prosecution then proceeds by issuing an *information*, which is a formal charging document similar to an indictment but without the time and effort of taking a case to the Grand Jury. This is another bargaining chip the defense attorney has in those jurisdictions where it is allowed.

• *Arraignment.* Once an indictment or information issues, the defendant will be summoned to court for an arraignment. The charges are read in open court, and the judge will ask the defendant for a plea. The defendant, in most cases, will plead not guilty and push the case on toward trial. In rare instances, the defendant will plead guilty, though that action is most often reserved for a later time.

Religious people sometimes get confused about the nature of a not-guilty plea. If they know they are guilty of the crime, they might consider it a lie to stand up in open court and say, "Not guilty." It is important to remember, though, that a plea of not guilty is not the same as saying, "I didn't do it!" This is little more than a step in the process, a way of moving the case along.

• *Hearings on Pre-Trial Motions.* Many of the remaining hearings prior to trial will involve motions filed by the lawyers—usually the defense attorney. The judge will accept legal briefs discussing these motions and sometimes will hear arguments before ruling. These motions include motions *in limine* (to exclude evidence such as forced confessions or items found during an illegal search), motions for dismissal (to end the case in the defendant's favor), and motions to compel (when one of the lawyers has failed to turn over documents or witness information as required by the rules of discovery). Your presence at these hearings is least important as they tend to be matters of law.

• *Fitness Hearing.*
Bart was a short fellow with a long, gray beard. He walked up

and down the streets each day, not seeming to be heading anywhere in particular. One day, Bart was arrested for striking a police officer. He said he thought the officer was trying to steal his ice-cream cone. After an investigation by the jail social worker, it was determined that Bart lived in the local SRO (single-room-only) hotel. The hotel management handled Bart's business and money after the closing of the mental institution in which he had been living. Bart's lawyer explained this to the judge, and Bart was released with only time served.

If a question arises as to the defendant's ability to understand the court process because of mental illness or lack of cognitive ability, a fitness hearing will be requested. First, the judge will appoint a mental health professional to evaluate the defendant. This might add several weeks to the case. Then, at the fitness hearing, if the psychiatrist testifies that a person is not competent to stand trial, that defendant will be taken to a mental hospital, ordered to undergo outpatient treatment, or have the entire case thrown out, depending on the nature of the crime (the mentally challenged, because of their difficulties, often do strange things that violate minor state or local laws). Barring those rare instances in which the case is dismissed, the defendant will remain in treatment for an indefinite period of time until he or she is deemed fit for trial, at which point the case will resume.

A fitness hearing is not the same as an *insanity defense*. Sometimes, a person's mental state can be so severely damaged that the individual no longer understands right from wrong or the consequences of his or her actions. In that case, the lawyer will offer an insanity defense which, if proven, will result in the defendant being found not guilty.

Depending on the case, the person might be released, or the judge could order commitment to an institution and treatment if the person remains a danger to self or others.

That, however, is a matter for trial. The fitness hearing is utilized merely for determining whether the defendant can comprehend what will happen as the cases moves forward.

DISCOVERY

At some point after the arraignment, the judge will set a date for the conclusion of discovery. Discovery is the legal process for turning over evidence between the parties to the case. In a criminal case, it mostly involves the prosecutor turning over evidence to the defense attorney. Prosecutors are not allowed to surprise the defense attorney and so must provide information about all physical evidence, witness statements, police reports, and anything else that might affect the outcome of a case.

The defense attorneys have to provide their evidence, but to a much lesser degree. For example, all conversations shared between the defendant and his or her lawyer are protected by attorney/client privilege, as is most information obtained by the lawyer's investigators. However, if the defense attorney comes into possession of key physical evidence such as the handgun believed to have been used in a homicide, this must be turned over. The defense attorney also must provide the prosecutor with a list of potential witnesses to be called.

Most of the time, a lawyer will not discuss options with you or your loved one before seeing the discovery evidence in order to understand what is likely to happen when the prosecution presents its case. Using this knowledge, the lawyer can help a defendant decide whether it will be better to have a trial or to accept a plea deal.

If the person is willing to consider pleading guilty, then the defense attorney will begin discussions with the prosecutor to negotiate the best possible outcome for both sides.

TRIAL

Defendants often become more anxious and agitated as the trial approaches. This can manifest as irritation, lack of cooperation, or changes in behavior. This is a natural reaction to a highly stressful situation as it draws closer to an end. Defendants might try to seem cool and under control, but they know their fate will be determined by others. You can help your loved one by being considerate, offering assurances of your support, and not adding pressure by getting angry yourself or dismissing his or her concerns. Keep in mind, you might be the only person with whom your loved one can communicate.

There are three options for a person facing a trial. First, the defendant can accept a plea agreement as discussed earlier. Second, every defendant has a right to a *jury trial* if he or she chooses. The third option is to ask for a *bench trial*. In the latter case, the trial will be conducted without a jury, and the judge alone rules on the question of guilt or innocence. Most cases end in either a plea bargain or a jury trial. Nonetheless, a bench trial could prove a viable option if the judge has a history of handling, understanding, or being lenient in certain types of cases. You or your loved one should discuss all of these options with the defense attorney. A local lawyer, especially, might have insight into the judge's history that can prove helpful.

In a jury trial, a panel of adult citizens (twelve in most states, though some jurisdictions use fewer) will be chosen from among a group of citizens already selected for jury duty during that term of court. Each potential juror is asked a series of questions by the lawyer for both sides. The questions are meant to uncover biases (beliefs that would sway the juror toward one side in a case regardless of the evidence). Biases often will cause a potential juror to be dismissed, as will the fact that an individual has seen or heard too much outside information about the case. Other people might be dismissed if they know the judge, lawyers, victim, defendant, arresting officer, or anyone that might be called as a witness.

After the jurors are selected, they are sworn in by the judge. They will be given initial instructions about what to expect during the trial, how to consider different types of evidence, how they should conduct themselves, and what they are prohibited from doing such as talking to the media or discussing the case outside the jury room. In a high-profile case, the jurors might be sequestered—that is, housed in a hotel under police protection to be certain no outside influences interfere with their decision-making process.

• *Opening Statements.* The trial begins with opening statements by both lawyers. Here the lawyers introduce the judge and/or the jury to the facts (as they see them) that they intend to prove during the trial. These statements are not considered as evidence, but they act more like the opening chapters of two separate mystery novels, one in which the main suspect is guilty, and one in which he or she is innocent.

- *The Prosecution's Case in Chief.* After the opening statements, the prosecution will put on its case in chief. This will include the testimony of witnesses—including expert witnesses (people paid to testify because of their expertise about a particular subject)—and the introduction of physical evidence. All witnesses will be cross-examined by the defense attorney.

- *Motion for Summary Judgment.* At the close of the prosecution's case, the defense attorney almost always makes a motion for summary judgment. This is a legal argument stating that the prosecution failed to prove its case. Such motions are standard practice and rarely granted by the judge. If the judge does rule in favor of the motion, however, a verdict of not guilty will be entered at this point and the case will end.

- *The Defense Case in Chief.* Assuming the judge has rejected the motion for summary judgement, the defense will put on its case, again possibly including witnesses and evidence. Keep in mind, however, that the defendant in a criminal case has a presumption of innocence, and it us up to the prosecutor to prove that person's guilt. Therefore, the defense is not required to put on any case at all. If the defense attorney believes the prosecution failed to prove guilt, then a strategic decision might be made not to introduce any evidence or testimony and instead to move on to the next step.

- *Rebuttal Case.* If the defense attorney chooses to call witnesses, then the prosecution will be allowed to call additional witnesses for the purpose of rebutting specific testimony—that is, countering that testimony with evidence or other witnesses. This will be a short and narrowly-focused portion of the trial. It also can be the part that might offer some surprises. Rebuttal witnesses are not part of the discovery process, and they are only called if needed. As such, what they have to say might not be clear until they take the witness stand.

• *Closing Arguments.* When all witnesses have testified and all the evidence has been presented, the prosecution and the defense will make their closing arguments. These monologues are not like the opening statements because in these the lawyers have a chance to spin the evidence in a way that makes sense for their versions of the story. Closing arguments can be powerful, blunt, and sometimes passionate. As with opening statements, though, they are not to be taken as evidence.

• *Jury Instructions.* The judge and both lawyers, through a series of discussions and legal arguments, will determine a set of instructions to give the jury. These include rules on how to view evidence, how to weigh some types of evidence against others, and what the jury must find in the evidence in order to convict a defendant on each possible charge. Once the instructions are determined, the judge will read them aloud to the jury.

• *Deliberations.* After the reading of the instructions, the jury is sent to the jury room where a foreman (leader) will be selected. The jurors then will consider all the evidence and attempt to reach a verdict (in most jurisdictions, a unanimous vote as to whether a person is guilty). While coming to a decision, the jurors may have questions which will be sent in writing to the judge, or they might wish to see particular pieces of evidence. Once a verdict is reached, the jurors will indicate this on a specific form.

• *Mistrial.* If the jury, after a reasonable amount of time and effort, is unable to reach a verdict, the judge will declare a mistrial. This doesn't end the case, but restarts it from the beginning. It will be up to the state's attorney whether to go through the process a second time.

• *The Verdict.* If a verdict has been reached, the judge will call all parties back to the courtroom and read the Verdict on the record. Then, if the verdict is guilty, the judge in most cases will order a pre-sentence investigation and set a date for sentencing.

At this point, if your loved one is on bond, the judge will decide whether to continue that bond or revoke it and return the person to jail.

If the defendant is acquitted by the jury—that is, found not guilty of the charges—then the case is over, and those charges can't be filed again. Your loved one will be released. Sometimes this will happen immediately, but on occasion a person might be taken back to the jail until all formal paperwork can be resolved.

SENTENCING

The sentencing phase begins with a pre-sentence investigation. This usually will be handled by a county probation officer or sheriff's deputy. It involves the collection of information, both positive and negative, about your loved one. Any prior criminal record will be included, as will statements from the victim or the victim's family, and any letters received advocating for leniency. At this point in the process, your efforts will be most valuable. Contact all the friends and family members that think well of your loved one and ask them to write letters. The judge will see all correspondence in the pre-sentence report, so the more letters sent on a person's behalf, the greater the chance of swaying the judge's sentiment.

The sentence imposed by the judge then will take one of several forms: 1) a determinate sentence (a specific number of years), 2) an indeterminate sentence (a time of incarceration between a minimum and a maximum number of years), 3) an alternative sentence (probation, home confinement, drug court, etc.), or 4) time served.

If the sentence seems especially long or harsh to you, keep in mind that your loved one likely won't serve the full amount of time. Most states have a system of *good time* in which an inmate earns days off a sentence for every day incarcerated without causing trouble. Good time can be anywhere from ten to fifty percent of a sentence, depending on the state. Also, most states allow the defense attorney to file a motion for reconsideration of sentence. When that is filed, if the judge doesn't dismiss it outright, your loved one will be brought back to court. At that point, the judge might choose to reduce the sentence or change it to either an alternative sentence or time served. Aside from these possibilities, any time before trial that your loved one spent on home confinement, in jail, or in drug rehab most likely will be deducted from the time left to serve.

APPEALS AND BEYOND

The court process will continue beyond the sentencing in the form of appeals to higher courts. This could take several years and go through various stages in multiple courts. Death-penalty cases especially can go on for many years. They begin with an automatic appeal to a higher court, and sometimes will end up in federal court and, ultimately, in the Supreme Court.

Some reasons for appeals have to do with legal technicalities. For example, there might have been errors made in the wording of a search warrant, the indictment, or the jury instructions. Any legal error made by the police, the prosecutor, or the judge can be grounds for an appeal. Also, a defendant might claim ineffective assistance of counsel. This happens when a defense attorney has failed to provide a defense considered reasonable by the standards of the average lawyer. Most of the time, ineffective-assistance-of-counsel claims fail, but not always. Plus, there have been blatant cases in which lawyers have come to court drunk or fallen asleep during testimony.

In recent years, many cases have been reversed because new technologies have provided proof of a person's innocence. DNA analysis alone has proven many people innocent of sometimes serious crimes. Before this type of evidence evaluation could take place, no clear form of proof was available to help these defendants.

Changes in understanding, public attitude, and laws also make a difference. Domestic violence is a perfect example of this. There have been many abused women who killed their husbands and, after being convicted and sentenced for murder, had their sentences thrown out or reduced because of our modern understanding of the effects of the abuse they suffered.

Lastly, in rare cases, state governors (or, in federal cases, the President) have issued pardons or commuted sentences.

This rarely happens because of political concerns, so many good reasons are needed to inspire such an action.

THE DEATH PENALTY: A PERSONAL CASE

Mention of the death penalty always reminds me of John Wayne Gacy Jr., the man referred to as the Killer Clown because he worked as a clown named Pogo at fundraisers and parties. Gacy was convicted in Illinois of sexually assaulting and murdering 33 young boys. He was executed by lethal injection on May 10, 1994.

Each time there was an execution at a local penitentiary, a small group I was involved with would meet outside the prison and pray for the dying person. Aside from our group, only a handful of other people would be there. The night of Gacy's execution was different. There were so many cars lined up along the sides of the major roads that I had to park a mile away and walk to the prison. I was alone as I walked, although everywhere I looked, there were police from many districts as well as lots and lots of people.

My group searched until we found an officer who let us go into a grassy area in front of the prison. This time, several hundred of us were praying, singing, and holding candles. Many people there were involved in the anti-death-penalty movement.

Hundreds of other folks had shown up for the spectacle. Most were young. Many were dressed as clowns. Some ran around hassling peaceful people, blowing out candles, and interfering with the songs and prayers of our group. Some shouted, "Die, clown! Die!" Quite a few taunted Gacy as if he could hear them through the prison walls. When the announcement came that Gacy had been executed, a lot of these people cheered.

I felt sad and uncomfortable as I made the long trek back to my car.

I admit that for many years I paid little attention to the death penalty. Even when one of my former students was given that sentence, I barely thought about it, although it saddened me.

Then I became a part of the National Convocation of Jail and Prison Ministries. One of the group's major concerns was the death penalty. Each year we met in a different major city across the country. Each year we marched against the death penalty. We even marched on the steps of the United States Capitol Building and the United States Supreme Court in Washington, D.C. Throughout that time as I learned more about the death penalty, my opposition to it grew.

These are the facts: 1) Most countries in the world no longer have the death penalty, and 2) some U.S. states *never* had it, while others have eliminated it over time.

While there are moral arguments against the death penalty, I always find that financial ones that impact all citizens are a better starting point. It costs three to four times more to utilize the death penalty than it does to keep a person in prison for life with no possibility of parole. The money for death-penalty cases is spent on years—sometimes decades—of court costs: judges, lawyers, paperwork, etc. It goes to extra security and separate housing for death-row inmates.

In addition to all this, victims' families must face years and years of mandatory appeals. They will have to make court appearances, and they will suffer uncertainty until the time comes for the execution. After that, if they have a change of heart or feel remorse and emptiness, it's too late to do anything about it.

Furthermore, every execution takes a toll on the administrators, staff, and inmates at the penitentiary as well.

It is not something easily dealt with and forgotten.

It is my opinion that the death penalty is a way out for the perpetrator of a crime. Death ends suffering, whereas life without parole would be an unending incarceration.

As if that weren't enough, life without mercy also avoids the execution of an innocent person. I attended a presentation several years ago in which more than 70 people spoke, all of whom had been convicted and sentenced to death but were later exonerated (proven not guilty). I can't forget how close these innocent people came to having their lives taken from them.

If someone in your life faces this terrible reality, don't try to deal with it alone. Find support. Get help from professional counselors. Expect this to be a long and stressful road. Do whatever you can, because your loved one needs you.

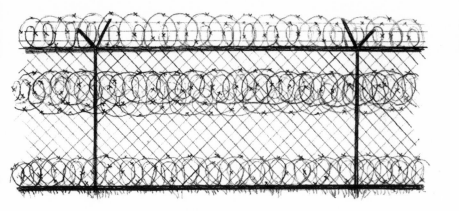

Part III.
Hard Time

THE STORIES OF ALEX AND CLARK

ALEX WAS A JOVIAL GUY in his mid-twenties. He enjoyed fun and good times with his many friends. He had gone to college—more than one—but failed to finish. Alex also did a good job working with his hands. He could do wood-working, welding, auto mechanics, and just about anything else he tried. He had spent a few years bouncing around between the family carpentry business and several other jobs. Then he told his family members that he was going into business for himself.

Unfortunately, the business Alex chose was illegal. He sold stolen car parts, equipment, and tools. They were supplied by one of his friends who trafficked in "hot" items. This job didn't work out for Alex. In only a few weeks, the local police caught on to what he was doing and arrested him.

Alex didn't have a lot of money, so his parents hired a good lawyer to represent him. The attorney worked hard to get the best deal possible from the prosecutor. After several months spent out of jail on bond, Alex accepted a plea agreement in which he pled guilty and received three years in prison.

Alex's family members were devastated by the news. His parents especially felt heartbroken and defeated. They visited him regularly during his incarceration.

Although he was a clever and adaptable guy, Alex hated his time in prison. At first, he blamed everyone—the government, his friends, his professors from college, and others—although he admitted that a major cause of his problems was greed.

It took time, but eventually Alex looked around and tried to figure out the best way to spend his three years in prison, during which he started out in one minimum-security facility and later was moved to another. Because he had some college experience, he became an assistant in the GED program, helping other inmates get their high-school-equivalency certificate. He said it passed the time.

Along the way, he learned a lot about the guys he was helping. Many of them lacked the financial advantages and strong family support that he enjoyed. It bothered him to realize that he had started out with a better chance in life than many of these guys, but he had squandered it.

So, Alex began to study college subjects just to keep busy. He also read a lot during the hours of lockdown. Slowly, his attitude changed. He began to plan for the future.

Alex was careful not to cause trouble or get bad reports during his time in prison, doing whatever he could to make sure he'd get out as soon as possible. When the opportunity presented itself, he made a bid to go to a work-release center near a major university. He was accepted and transferred. Once there, he found a job as a lab assistant at the university, which allowed him to utilize his mechanical skills. He enrolled in school as well and worked toward earning his degree in science.

When his time in work release was finished, Alex found a small apartment in the area, kept his job, and finished up the coursework for his degree.

The next move in his life was for him to return to his home town. He found an apartment and a good industry job. He enjoyed the work.

Alex's parents were proud of him. They had been with him through the entire process, sometimes feeling as if they, too, were in prison. Now they got to see and experience the rewards of this. Alex interacted with them regularly, while also falling in love with a nice woman, whom he married. He soon moved back to the university town after receiving a teaching fellowship, which meant he could teach college and earn his Master's degree at the same time. When this concluded, he continued to teach and work in the laboratory. He went on to earn a doctorate.

Alex not only changed his attitude, he changed his life.

Not all prisoners have the success that Alex did. The support of his parents and other family members was critical to his finding himself during incarceration. Without their love and encouragement, he likely would have seen himself as just another convict, hopeless and alone. Because they were there for him, however, Alex was able to achieve great things.

Unfortunately, this is the exception, not the rule. Clark's story shows the other side.

Clark grew up in the suburbs. Both of his parents were alive, but neither took a particular interest in his life. He joined a gang early on and, though he was capable and intelligent, dropped out of high school in the middle of his sophomore year. He ended up in juvenile detention several times for charges that included gang activities, theft, battery, and drug sales. After he turned eighteen, he picked up similar charges twice, both times being sentenced to the penitentiary.

During his time in prison, he was able to obtain whatever drugs he wanted and stayed high much of the time. His parents never visited, and he rarely spoke to them on the phone. Instead, he spent his time with his gang friends. Clark ignored GED and other school programs because he thought that, if he attended them, the gang guys would see this as a weakness and betrayal. He became more involved with gang activity as time passed. He learned a lot of schemes and scams and became proficient at lying.

Each time Clark was released from prison, he made contact with his family and promised them that he'd never go back. He planned to find a job and start working.

It never quite worked out. Clark's friends always found out he was back in town. They called him and, sometimes, knocked on his door. They kept at it until he gave in to their desires and went out with them to celebrate. That led to more frequent contacts. Then, soon, he returned to his negative behaviors.

The end of Clark's story isn't good. Overdose, drive-by shooting, street fight, automobile accident—the cause of his death isn't important. What matters is that he died before he could turn thirty.

Most people sent to prison won't have the extreme successes or failures as seen in the stories of Alex and Clark. Even so, the outcome is never guaranteed. Many factors determine this, including the support of loved ones, the person's willingness to change and better him/herself, and the nature of the facility in which the incarceration takes place. Some prisons are safe, while others aren't. Some offer beneficial programs—education, substance abuse counseling, mental health care, reentry assistance—whereas others don't. Some are violent places where drug use is rampant and a person's safety can't be assured, but others provide a stable, secure place to serve out a sentence. In addition to this, the person also bears a lot of responsibility for his or her rehabilitation. Some individuals are ready to change, and others aren't. Unfortunately, this isn't a simple problem, and no easy solution exists.

The important thing is for you to be there to listen to your loved one's concerns, whether through visitation or over the telephone. Try to provide guidance without judgment or criticism.

Most prisoners will do their time and return to society. A few, however, will be physically injured, while a smaller number will die in fights, riots, from illness, or for other reasons. If you're there for your loved one, you will know when problems arise and can help in dealing with them.

No broad statement can be made about prisons, because each tends to be different from others. A well-run maximum-security institution, for example, might be safer than a poorly-run minimum-security facility. Regardless of what you see in movies and on television, most modern prisons have a good safety record. The staff and correctional officers will do their best to ensure no one is hurt. At the same time, you will have no say in where your loved one ends up.

Once a person is moved to a penitentiary or correctional center, it is easy to find out about the place by doing research online. Also, never hesitate to ask your loved one for descriptions of what life there is like. Sometimes, just telling the story can be helpful and relieve a person's stress.

Being in any kind of prison is a negative experience. Freedom, choices, and a control of a person's life are taken away. Spending every day with others in the same situation often leads to tension, anger, and anxiety, both for the inmates and staff. Even the most balanced people feel the negative psychological effects of incarceration. In addition, a large percentage of the prison population (twenty percent or more) suffers from some form of mental illness.

Don't lose hope for your loved one. It *is* possible for a person to return to society and succeed as Alex did. Sometimes it just takes a little growing up. Often, a genuine religious experience will turn a person around. For other folks, time alone to think and reflect has more of an impact. Twelve-step programs such as Alcoholics Anonymous and Narcotics Anonymous could be the catalyst for change. In some states, prisons are designed around the Boot Camp experience, meant to alter life patterns and build self-esteem. What works for one person might not work for another, but options do exist. There is no way to know when or why a person will change unless that person shares the reason with you. Your loved one alone will have to find ways to survive and flourish inside the prison walls.

All you can do is be available and offer support whenever it's needed.

A CLASH OF CULTURES

Blanche, a prison staffer, lost her clerical job because she did things in the order she wanted instead of what was expected. She failed to finish reports before their deadline because she spent too much time talking to the inmate assistant assigned to the office where she worked.

The Rev. Humphry was refused entry into the prison after he took an inmate's mail out of the facility without first sending it through the proper channels.

Lola, a prison cook, was arrested for shoplifting at a local convenience store. She was immediately dismissed.

One of the inmates, Duke, was wealthy, well known, and politically connected. He convinced an officer to bring him meals from outside the prison. When this was discovered, details hit the local newspapers. Both Duke and the officer received punishment for this breach.

Monroe developed a strategy for committing criminal acts while he was incarcerated. He would get information about individuals and use that to force them to assist him in his illegal activities. Monroe also would call a store and get the name of the person who answered. At the facility where Monroe was locked up, the inmates had some access to the internet, so he would look up information about the store employee in order to learn her home address. Then he would call the store again and demand money from the woman, threatening to harm her and her family if she didn't comply.

Virgil never committed infractions while in prison. He didn't get the chance. A former local police officer who had been convicted for armed robbery, Virgil was placed in a solitary cell in the administrative segregation unit. It was for his protection. Other inmates might have held grudges or sought revenge against him because of his time as a cop. He had arrested several of the other prisoners.

There is no easy way to explain the tensions and difficulties within institutions that incarcerate people. These facilities are so different in purpose, size, administration, operations, etc., that no simple, general comments can adequately express what goes on in each. Some things, however, are similar: the various cultures that develop inside a prison. Trying to understand these might help you to get a better grasp on why this shadowy world can be so difficult to describe.

First, there is a *culture of incarceration* that separates correctional employees from inmates, sometimes resulting in people from one side not viewing people from the other as human beings. It stems from the control relationship between staff and prisoners. The administrators and staff have all the power.

Administrators usually are well educated and have worked their way up to their positions. Their responsibilities are to follow the letter of the law, protect the external community, and enforce the institutional rules while also protecting the inmates and treating them humanely. At the same time, there often will be internal politics at play between those seeking advancement, as well as external politics in which the wardens and administrators are accountable to state and county officials elected or appointed at the highest levels.

The staffers and correctional officers vary more in their backgrounds, education, experience, etc. Their training and titles are often militaristic. The officers, especially, follow the military system by a structure of rank: officer, corporal, sergeant, lieutenant, captain, etc. Some of them are trained at police academies. Theirs is a dangerous job. As such, officers are taught to keep their distance from the inmates as much as possible. Because the staffers and prisoners spend so much time together, however, this can be difficult.

Various other employees and volunteers include the kitchen staff (usually individuals sent in by an outside company with a contract to supply meals for that institution), road crew bosses, commissary managers, counselors, chaplains, and teachers. They also have rules to follow, and they are encouraged not to become close to individual prisoners or provide services beyond their specific duties.

The culture of incarceration is such that inmates will try to get close to individual staffers or even correctional officers in order to gain something from them. Drugs, tobacco, money, and sex are the usual motivators, but even a fresh slice of pizza can be a cherished prize for an inmate that hasn't tasted one in many years. Because of this, the rituals of courtship between an inmate and a staffer can be quite calculated, even when they might seem smooth and spontaneous.

The next thing to consider is the *culture of special circumstances.* Famous people, politicians, folks with a lot of media coverage, wealthy individuals, and various others might ask for and sometimes receive special considerations. Often, this will be for their own protection as in the case of Virgil above. Former police officers are usually given more secure and less visible placement, as are dangerous criminals, people who have served as confidential informants, and similar individuals who might be at a higher risk if placed in the general population.

The staff also must make accommodations for folks with physical disabilities. In many facilities, cells on the first floor of each living area will be set aside for inmates who use wheelchairs, are prone to epileptic seizures, or have some other medical concern that requires them to be at ground level or close to the main gate on a pod.

Next, there is a *culture of gangs.* Racial issues that might be less common and concealed outside prison walls are prevalent and exposed in the penitentiary. Many gangs exist in prison, including the familiar ones such as Bloods, Crips, and Aryans.

In some facilities, these gangs, because of their numbers and their willingness to stick together, wield a certain amount of power. Violence and control are their tools, and many use hatred of other races as a bonding tool.

Also, individuals from the same geographic area sometimes band together into gangs. These, you might be able to spot by jailhouse tattoos of their local zip or area codes.

Other groups form by default. These are not necessarily gangs. One group might be made up of the inmates that mind their own business. Others might form around activities such as chess, board and card games, music, sports, exercise, etc.

As you see, there are a lot of dynamics that determine what your loved one's prison experience will be like: the personalities of staff and other inmates, limitations of space, the rules of the institution, issues of race, and various other factors will force your loved one to adapt.

Difficulties can arise in many ways. If you feel your loved one is in jeopardy, you should encourage him or her to contact a counselor, the chaplain, or other staffer who might be able to resolve the situation. However, the reality of prison life is that most inmates won't take this step for fear of being labeled a "rat" or a "snitch." As such, you might have to contact the prison yourself.

Most facilities have a section for inmates placed in protective custody or administrative segregation. This might be the best solution, but it also should be the last option because it will affect your loved one's situation for the rest of his or her time in prison.

PROCESSING CENTERS
AND CLASSIFICATION FACILITIES

In many states, inmates are not taken directly from jail to prison. Instead, they go to an interim location called alternately a processing center or a classification facility. This unit might be a stand-alone building or a part of another prison or jail that is kept isolated from the rest of the inmate population.

Your loved one likely will be transferred to such a facility without prior notice, taking little aside from whatever funds remain on his or her inmate trustee account. During the first few days, new arrivals are kept in isolation and on total lockdown. As such, they will have no access to a telephone. You might not hear from your loved one for several days because of this. If you start to feel concerned about why a person hasn't called you, check the state prison website first. It will keep you updated about your loved one's whereabouts.

What happens inside a classification center? Your loved one will be placed in the system based on determinations made here. This is where people receive their prison numbers and identification cards. Their identities are confirmed, court papers evaluated, and discharge and parole eligibility dates set. They will have their tattoos and scars catalogued. Most folks will receive orientation (sometimes just a packet of information to read or a video to watch), testing for I.Q. and psychological issues, and various health exams (physical, mental, optical, etc.). Any medicines needed will be prescribed or continued. In addition, evaluations will be made to determine a person's educational and vocational needs as well as what correctional programs he or she will be required to take (classes about substance abuse, sexual abuse, parenting, anger management, etc.). All of these steps are taken for the purpose of determining 1) a person's classification or risk level, and 2) to what long-term facility that person will be transferred.

Placement of an inmate depends on the nature of the crime committed, the length of the sentence (the term ordered by the judge and also that part of the term remaining to be served), a person's past criminal record, and other factors. Maximum security and Super-max placement are for those who have extremely long sentences, prior escape attempts, histories of violent or aggressive behavior, or a record of causing serious trouble in the system. Minimum security is for those with non-violent crimes, short sentences, a history of good behavior, and a release or parole eligibility date in the near future. Some states also have medium security facilities, to which the majority of inmates are sent.

You need to understand that placement within the system has little to do with the outside residence of a person. In fact, for a federal crime, a person might be transferred to a facility all the way on the other side of the country.

If you have a serious, well-documented hardship or medical reason, you might be able to get your loved one transferred closer to home, but again, such an issue must be extreme and verifiable. If this is a situation that applies to you, you might contact your local legislator. Or, in some states it will be a simple matter of filling out paperwork for the Department of Corrections.

OTHER TYPES OF PRISONS

In addition to those facilities already mentioned, there are ICE and for-profit prisons. Your loved one might not encounter these, but you should be aware of them.

As mentioned earlier, ICE stands for *Immigration and Customs Enforcement*, which is an agency of the U.S. government. ICE facilities hold people who, for whatever reason, are to be returned to their countries of origin. ICE is overseen by the Office of Homeland Security. It does investigations and enforcement under federal statutes and has more than 200 detention facilities nationwide.

There are mainly two types of prisoners held in ICE detention: those being deported because of criminal activities, and those being evaluated to determine whether they will be returned to their countries of origin because of immigration irregularities (they entered the U.S. illegally, overstayed their visas, lied on applications for entry, etc.).

Deportation can be a complicated and lengthy process. It involves treaties and agreements between the U.S. and other countries. If no treaty exists, then a third country must be found that will accept the person being deported, and this is not always feasible. As such, some ICE inmates might be detained for an indefinite period of time. Gaining release for a person in that situation can seem impossible, and your only hope is to find a good lawyer.

Foreign nationals convicted of crimes in the U.S. might serve their time here or be deported immediately. If serving out their time in the U.S., some might be transferred to a traditional prison and then moved to an ICE facility after discharging their sentence.

The laws for holding ICE detainees are different from those for U.S. citizens. ICE detainees don't get the benefit of many rights granted under the U.S. Constitution. Lawyers might not be provided, or translators available. Access to family and friends often is restricted. Adults and children, criminals and detainees sometimes are housed in the same facilities and later transported together. Furthermore, there is a lack of transparency, so a family might have no idea where a loved one is or whether he or she already has been deported.

The other type of prison—becoming more common of late—is the for-profit prison. These are run by private companies for financial gain. They provide incarceration services to various jurisdictions. Sometimes these aren't even in the state where your loved one is incarcerated. If a particular state has a prison overcrowding problem, that state might contract with a for-profit prison in another state to house inmates.

What is important to remember about for-profit prisons is that they must abide by the rules for management and prisoner discipline established by the sentencing state's Department of Corrections and grant inmates the rights and privileges of the sentencing state's Constitution. However, these facilities might have their own additional rules as well. Prisons will provide their inmates with a rulebook, so your loved one needs to learn the rules.

INMATE PROPERTY AND MAIL

In the rulebook your loved one is given, there will be a list of all personal items that an inmate in that facility may possess. Anything not on the list, not belonging to person in possession of it, or that is being used in a manner other than that for which it was intended will be considered contraband and could result in disciplinary action.

Most institutions provide uniforms and other clothing, although in some facilities (work-release centers, for example), clothes are the responsibility of the individual and must follow the institution's guidelines. Even where these items are provided, additional clothing items might be permitted. These items include sweatshirts and sweatpants, sneakers, thermal underwear, and in some places, hats or wristwatches. Inmates either will be allowed to purchase those items from the commissary or order them from specifically designated companies or catalogues, again as determined by facility rules. While you might be permitted to order these things for an inmate from one of the selected catalogues, personally sending your loved one items isn't permitted.

The same is true with books. Most places allow you to order books for your loved one. However, different institutions have different rules as to how you do it. Some might permit books only from the book's publisher or a particular store, while others might require that they come from a faceless entity such as Amazon.com in which the chances of contraband being smuggled by being hidden inside the books is lessened.

Magazine subscriptions are permitted in most places. However, they must not include pornography, pictures and descriptions of weapons, or inappropriate topics such as lock-picking or how to cook crystal meth.

Some prisons also allow inmates to possess radios, TVs, computers, musical instruments, or other large items. Again, check the rulebook.

If you wish to send your loved one money, you might need to call the facility to find out the procedure for this. In almost all cases, you can send a money order (or sometimes a cashier's check, though never a personal check) by mail. Even then, different institutions have different rules for how these must be filled out. If those rules aren't followed precisely, the money order will be returned (usually at the cost to the inmate of a stamp and an envelope). Some places might take in-person cash deposits if you happen to be visiting that day, but you will need to ask a staff member whether this is so. More and more prisons also now allow electronic transfers online through Western Union or a similar company. You can log on to the prison's website to find out if this is the case and what you need to do.

That brings up the subject of your loved one's mail. Various federal courts have ruled that an inmate, except in rare circumstances such as punitive segregation, has a right to send and receive mail. The courts have further noted that, while an inmate might lose many of his or her rights, you as a free citizen have not lost yours. As such, no prison can reasonably refuse to allow your mail to be delivered to an inmate. What each institution can and does do is set rules about what types of mail will be permitted. Plain birthday cards might be okay, for example, but not ones with glitter on them or voice recordings. Photographs likely will have to meet certain standards of decency. Some prisons require all letters to be handwritten, while others allow typescript or computer printouts. This information also should be in the rulebook. If it isn't, call the facility to find out what you need to know.

Your loved one will be grateful for any mail received.

Inmates often spend a great deal of their time responding to letters. It allows them to pass the seemingly endless hours. If you aren't a good correspondent, sometimes just a note that says "thinking of you" or a humorous card might satisfy loved ones to let them know they haven't been forgotten.

Whenever you send mail, keep in mind that all letters will be opened and in many cases read by mailroom staff at the facility, and the envelopes will be checked for contraband. Stamps, envelope closures, etc., will be removed because in the past they have been used to hide drugs. For that same reason, never use highlighters, magic markers, or stickers (even address labels will be detached), and don't kiss the envelope with lipstick or spray it with perfume.

WARNING: If you are asked to forward a letter to someone in another institution, don't do it. Letters from someone in one facility to someone in another must be approved by the wardens of both places. Your loved one could get in trouble for this, and you might lose your visitation privileges the same way you would if you violated a rule while at the facility in person.

DELIVERING BAD NEWS

A correctional officer called the office of the prison social worker and asked for someone to come and talk to an inmate named Barry. Barry's wife just told him that their marriage was over and she was filing for divorce.

When the social worker arrived, she found Barry sitting on the floor in the video visitation area. She told the officer she intended to sit on the floor in front of Barry as she spoke to him.

The officer agreed and monitored the conversation through a closed-circuit TV camera.

The social worker spent some time with Barry until he was willing to stand up. She helped him look realistically at the situation.

Though hurting inside, Barry calmed down and was able to return to his cell.

Throughout the rest of Barry's stay, the social worker met with him regularly and helped him to cope with life after divorce.

Sharing bad news about relationships, deaths, financial disasters, illnesses, negative court results, etc., is never easy. The first thing you should know is that, although you need not reveal every detail of a situation, it is important that you never lie. Trust is one of the most important issues for prisoners. You don't want to destroy that trust in you. If you withhold important information or lie about it, your loved one will find out eventually, maybe from someone else. Even if it can be kept a secret until the person is released from the penitentiary, the truth will come out. Then he or she will resent you for it. By telling the story up front and letting a person get used to the idea, your loved one will be better prepared when the time comes for release. That period of transition will be hard enough without negative surprises.

Besides, you are your loved one's connection to the world outside the prison walls. You provide the news, even if it causes distress. An inmate is still human, experiencing human emotions and curiosity. He or she needs to know the good things as well as the bad.

Sometimes you will be able to tell when trouble is coming and so warn your loved one. Other times, you won't. Each situation will need its own approach.

The best way to deal with delivering bad news is to plan ahead. Figure out what you will say, how you intend to say it, and how much information you are willing to share. You might choose to tell the person immediately or you might wait until you can talk face to face. Your approach should depend on the situation, the inmate, and you. When you do speak to the person, give him or her time to ask questions and make comments, then to cool down and face the reality you have just shared. Carefully observe the person's reaction and, while doing so, be prepared to deal with tears, anger, silence, violent outbursts, and a host of other displays of emotion. When concluding, ask if there is anything you can do. Then end by sharing your plans, especially informing the person if and when you intend to make contact again.

If this is about a death in the family, be sure to send anything your loved one might find important such as the obituary, the prayer card, the order of the service, the location of the burial if there is one, names of those who attended the funeral, etc. It might even help to send a picture of the deceased that was taken at a happier time.

In the case of a divorce or breakup, the person needs to know that the change is real and that there is nothing more to discuss about the decision. Negotiations regarding property or children's issues can be handled later after the initial shock has worn off.

Illnesses and financial difficulties might be on-going and therefore will need to be faced again and again as situations change. The same is true for legal issues involving other members of the family.

If you believe your loved one might react violently or attempt suicide, inform the officer in charge or the social worker. You also may contact the warden's office or the Watch Commander immediately if you believe the situation warrants it and the danger is close at hand. In either case, the prison staff will make sure the person is handled appropriately (the inmate is placed on suicide watch or in administrative segregation, for example).

If the person reacts negatively, try not to let it upset you. Remember, you are the messenger of bad news. That doesn't mean you are the cause of it.

VISITATION

Visiting an inmate in prison usually will be for a longer amount of time than in a jail setting. However, as with visiting in jail, you should learn the rules before you go. Many will be the same (dress appropriately, for example). Others might seem odd. Whatever the case, all are designed to keep the facility safe and free of contraband.

Out of all the rules you will encounter, the most important one is this: *no matter how much your loved one pleads with you, never bring contraband into the facility.* That should be obvious, but it nonetheless needs to be said. Likewise, *don't have drugs or guns in your vehicle.* People are arrested far too often at prisons and in prison parking lots for having weapons, drugs, alcohol, and other contraband. Even if your loved one has a headache, don't bring an aspirin. These are simple rules, and violating them can carry charges that carry jail or prison time.

Along those same lines, understand beforehand that your belongings will be searched. You will be patted down. You will have to walk through a metal detector or be scanned with a detection wand. Many facilities won't allow you to bring jewelry, keys, purses, or money into the visitation area (though some places will allow a few dollar bills or coins for use in vending machines). Your best bet is to take as little as possible.

Do take two forms of identification, at least one of them with your picture on it. This is the same as when visiting at a jail. The results will be the same as well: if you have any outstanding warrants, you will be arrested.

Despite the strict security measures, remember that you are entitled to be treated with courtesy, although it won't happen in all cases. Prison staff members have bad days just like you do, and some have seemingly gruff personalities as with many of the folks you might meet in your day-to-day life. Plus, they have duties to perform. Try not to be disrespectful in return. Besides, you never know what is happening inside the prison on any particular day. There might have been a fight, or else the facility could be in the midst of cell-by-cell search for contraband, either of which might cause visitation to be suspended.

If you are refused a visit or some other incident happens, it is best for you to leave quickly and quietly. Make a note of the time this happened as well as the names of any staff members involved. You can deal with it by writing to the administration later. While you do have the immediate recourse to ask for a supervisor, sometimes confrontation is not a good idea at a time when your emotions might be overflowing.

Often, prison visitation rules will seem like an annoyance. If, however, something comes up for which you need an exception to one of the rules, you must get this cleared *prior* to the visit by contacting the administration. Keep in mind that your reason for requesting such an exception must be serious and genuine. Exceptions are rarely made.

Plan ahead also if you are bringing children to a visit. Even babies will be searched (people have used children and child carriers for smuggling contraband into prisons). Also, there will be a waiting period between check-in and the actual visit, so bring something for the kids to do. If you have kids, you already know that they can be fussy.

Each child reacts differently upon entering the prison environment. You and your loved one need to be prepared for whatever happens. Kids can get angry, sad, afraid, etc., just like adults, and often much more visibly. Sometimes they respond in outbursts of screaming, crying, or causing trouble. Prepare the children ahead of time so that they know what to expect. Also, be sure that they understand that your loved one can't go home with them.

For adults *and* children, the hardest part of the visit comes when it is time to leave. Plan how to exit on a positive note. You always want to assure your loved one that you care. Certain signs of affection such as a brief hug or a chaste kiss might be permitted, depending on the institution. Some families, regardless of their religious beliefs, take a moment to pray. Do what feels right to you.

The other important thing is to keep coming back. The prison experience might last for many years, and your loved one needs you. Schedule your visits carefully and as often as you can.

SOLITARY CONFINEMENT

Solitary confinement was once considered a short-term punishment for violent acts. Through the years, as more institutions with single cells were built, more people were impacted and for a longer time. It can be either punitive or administrative segregation and usually involves the inmate being locked down for 23 hours per day and having little or no contact with other residents or even correctional officers. Time in solitary is usually brief when punishing an inmate for rule violations, but in extreme cases where administrative segregation is required (the inmate is considered a danger to him/herself or others, is in danger from other prisoners, or is on Death Row) the solitary confinement can last for extended periods. Some individuals have spent years alone. This isolated and negative existence can even lead to mental illness for some people. Usually they get no phone calls, no visits, no packages and no commissary. Even clergy visits may be restricted. A few states are re-examining this issue, but changes come slowly to the prison system.

If your loved one is in some form of solitary confinement, all you can do is continue to send letters and cards. You may decide to send them more frequently. If you don't get a response, do not stop sending them. This may be the inmate's only lifeline.

You might want to ask the counselor, chaplain or even the warden why this person is in solitary and how long it will last. You definitely should alert the inmate's lawyer about this situation (lawyers are the only people that can't be refused if they desire to speak with an inmate).

If you suspect your loved one has or is developing mental health issues, let the institution know you are concerned about his or her wellbeing. Be sure to keep copies of your letters and the administration's responses, dates of phone calls, and other data. This may not bring about any changes but it will let staff at the institution know that this person has support on the outside.

DEATH ON THE INSIDE

Darnell was convicted of a serious crime and was sentenced to several years in prison. He had a number of medical issues and was sent to a facility with a good medical unit. Even there, he died after only a couple of years.

Darnell's family lacked the funds to bury him. The state contracted with a local funeral home and cemetery. No real service was held, but Darnell was buried with dignity.

When Elmer died after a long illness, his family made arrangements for a church service and burial at the family cemetery. Elmer's wife and mother were there, along with other relatives. The two of them had control of the service and other details.

Although most people finish their sentences and leave prison, some do die on the inside. This could be from natural causes, violence, or on occasion, suicide. The cause of death will be determined and placed on the death certificate as is done anywhere else. You will want copies of that death certificate. You need them to handle insurance claims, transfers and sales of property, as well as any unresolved legal proceedings.

If your loved one is seriously ill, you can prepare for his or her death by keeping informed. To do this, you must go through the social worker and/or the medical unit to learn about the person's health. Because of privacy laws in the United States, the inmate might have to sign permission forms to allow you to receive such information. However, if your loved one is incapacitated, you might need to contact a lawyer and go before a judge, or possibly have a guardian *ad litem* appointed to represent the person's interests.

Depending on your loved one's crime and the nature of his or her illness, it might be possible to secure release. Some states have what is referred to as *compassionate release* or *medical release*. If a person is in the last stages of a terminal illness or might not live without a specific treatment that the prison can't provide, the inmate might be granted a compassionate release. While this rarely happens, you should look into it. It will involve forms being filled out and forwarded to either the governor or the parole board (depending on the state), which will make a final determination. Also, your loved one's lawyer can file a motion for reconsideration to be handled by the sentencing judge, citing the terminal illness as grounds. As such, the judge might release your loved one out of compassion. However, this, too, is a rare occurrence.

More likely, your loved one will spend his or her last days in the medical unit. Some institutions do have hospice for people in palliative care (care for those diagnosed as unlikely to live for more than a year). Others transport dying inmates to a hospital where they will remain under guard until the end.

Every jurisdiction has different procedures. Contact the administration. You need to ask questions and find out what will be done.

DEATH ON THE OUTSIDE

Vera, a woman in her sixties, was the only person in contact with her incarcerated son, Elton. She was a source of comfort and support for him. "If I die," Vera said, "Elton will have no one left that cares what happens to him." She started making plans, just in case.

Everyone dies eventually. We are, all of us, fragile human beings, and our time will come when we least expect it. This is something we don't want to think about, but it is reality.

Losing someone can be hard enough, but for those behind prison walls, it goes beyond mere grief. If you, like Vera, are supporting someone who is incarcerated, now would be a good time to pause and consider what that person's life might be like should something happen to you. Have you made plans for that possibility? Will someone else visit the person in prison, take collect calls, or send money? If you are a person's only contact, now is the time to figure these things out. Otherwise, what happens if you should pass away suddenly or become so infirm that you can't do the normal day-to-day things?

Who could you ask to take your place in your loved one's life? Ideally, that role would be filled by a relative or acquaintance. If you have anyone in mind, sit down with him or her and discuss the possibility. A good suggestion is to have that person go ahead and make contact with your incarcerated loved one. Perhaps the two of them can exchange letters or maybe phone calls. Any contact will prepare both for what to expect should something bad happen.

If you don't have anyone willing to do this, contact your church or community center. Ask if there is an individual or a group willing to fill in for you should it become necessary.

Another thing to do as preparation is to update your will so that your loved one will be taken care of in the event of your death. You might want to leave that person some money so that prison and commissary needs are met. However, it wouldn't be advisable to leave *too much* money, because that might make the inmate a target for unscrupulous people. Ask your lawyer about setting up a trust so that a small amount of money will be sent every month, instead of having it all sent at one time.

Be sure your loved one has a picture of you, and of other close family members as well. That seems like a small detail, but it can mean a lot.

Also, it is a good idea for you to write a letter and make arrangements for it to be mailed in the event of your passing. Tell the person how important he or she has been in your life. Put down a few positive memories. Recall funny and happy times. You might also share a poem, a reading, a book, a song, or some other remembrance. To a loved one in prison, such a letter would be a treasure.

MARRIAGE

Iris was on the radio. She began her segment by saying, "Some people meet their soulmates in an incarcerated setting." Iris's was an interesting story. She had a ministry at one of the local prisons, but she gave that up to marry one of the inmates. She had fallen in love with the man. To her, marriage seemed like the right thing to do.

Aside from a death in the family, there are other life-changing events that can happen for a prisoner. One of these things is to get married. To the average person, thinking of anyone marrying an inmate might seem shocking. The truth is, most prisons see at least two or three weddings each year, and in some facilities, many more.

Sometimes the inmate and betrothed knew each other before the one went to prison. They might have been living together. Other times, the two have met recently, either through correspondence or after being introduced by someone else. Perhaps the two people love each other, or maybe they have other motives. Regardless, once two people decide to get married, in the majority of cases, the state will allow it.

We all have a variety of motivations in most actions we take. Many men tend to be more practical, while many women have a more romantic point of view. Idealy the guiding motivation for two people getting married is their love for each other. This, however, is not always the case. Maybe for your friend or family member, it is. Understanding your loved one's state of mind and how he or she sees the relationship will help you decide.

Looking at motivation, people on the inside might be seeking security. They might want someone to send a little extra money every month. They might be trying to create a good image for the judge or parole board. They might want a commitment to keep the other person from seeking different companions. They might be considering a place to go upon release.

The motivation of the person on the outside could be as a crusader who expects to change or save the inmate. This person might be a thrill-seeker who picked a prisoner's name off a web site and began to correspond. Perhaps this person is lonely and has been unsuccessful at finding a partner. This could even be someone who just wants to be the focus of attention.

Getting to know the other person is important, not just for your loved one, but for you as well. Ask to be put in contact. Meet up with this potential new member of the family. Spend some time getting to know him or her. Perhaps the two of you can form a bond that will help in the future. Or, in the worst case, maybe you will need to cut ties with both people once the situation becomes clear. Either way, try not to prejudge. Be polite, but also be straightforward.

Of course, there is the possibility *you* are the one marrying an inmate. Maybe you have had a long relationship. Perhaps you even have children together. If you do, know in advance that there will be many ups and downs, especially if your loved one is serving a long sentence.

A note of warning: if you have young children and the inmate has been convicted of a sex offense, please understand that you might be placing your family in danger. Think of the best interests of the children first, because that is what the courts will do should a later issue arise and a judge have to decide whether you get to keep custody of your own kids.

Finally, one practical concern. If you are marrying an inmate, only the minister, you as the spouse-to-be, and perhaps a couple of witnesses will be allowed to attend. Each person must go through a process of screening much like that for any visitor to the facility. Former employees of the prison or recent inmates in any facility might not be permitted. That includes *you*. On arrival, every person allowed to attend will be searched, just like on visitation days.

After that, each facility's rules are different, so you will want to learn more about what will happen. The prison's chaplain should be able to fill you in on all the details.

A LONG ROAD

This has been a brief look at what you will experience while dealing with the incarceration of a friend or family member. There are many other things that an inmate goes through, some that you will learn about in time, and others that you might never know. Disciplinary actions against inmates, for example, are things many prisoners choose not to discuss. Instances of intimidation, fist fighting, or even sexual assault are also possible in prison, though much less common than the average prison movie would indicate. Your loved one could experience trouble because of gambling with other inmates or trading commissary for tobacco or drugs that have been smuggled into the facility.

There are positive things as well. Some prisons allow you to order holiday packages of grocery items from specific companies. Others have a monthly take-out night for inmates on good behavior in which your loved one might be able to order a pizza or a sack of fast-food hamburgers as long as there is money in his or her trustee account.

Whatever the case, the best thing you can do is listen to your loved one and ask questions whenever something comes up. If the person doesn't want to talk about it, never get angry, but let him or her know that you are there to listen when needed and will help if you can.

For you and your loved one, this is a long road, and prison

isn't the end of it. There will be much more to deal with after the prison walls have receded in your rearview mirror for the last time.

Part IV.
Coming Home

RELEASE

TOTAL FREEDOM COMES WHEN INMATES have served their entire term of incarceration. They are said to have *discharged* their sentence. However, the majority of prisoners are released prior to discharge. That is the government's way of freeing up prison space while still keeping an eye on convicted felons that have hit the streets. There are a variety of ways in which early release occurs:

• *Parole.* A person is released into the supervision of a parole officer. This will involve meetings with the parole officer, as well as the officer visiting the parolee's residence and work site. There will be regular drug and alcohol testing, and sometimes a psychological evaluation. The parolee is expected to report to the parole officer immediately upon release, and then periodically to discuss progress and concerns. In some states, the parolee will have a curfew, and the parole officer will make spot checks or phone calls late at night to confirm the person's whereabouts. If the parolee is on intensive parole or electronic monitoring, the interactions with the parole officer will be more exacting.

Parole usually lasts a minimum of a year. If the parolee stays out of trouble, follows the rules, and doesn't fail a drug or alcohol test, then he or she will be eligible for a discharge of sentence. However, the period of parole can last much longer, and a person will be expected to pay off fines, court costs, and court-ordered restitution prior to being discharged from parole.

How can you help your loved one? He or she will need transportation to the parole office as well as back and forth to work. Getting fired from a job or failing to show up for an appointment with the parole officer often are grounds to have the parole immediately revoked and the parolee sent back to prison. Also, keep in close contact with your loved one and watch for signs that he or she is falling back into old habits such as using drugs or hanging around with known criminals.

• *Work Release.* This is a transitional program available to some nonviolent offenders. They are technically still in the custody of the state, and the facility in which they are staying might have a name that ends with Correctional Center or Work Release Center, but the people sent here dress in normal clothes and are out of the facility for much of the day to work at regular jobs. The best way for you to help a loved one in a work-release program is to provide information about possible jobs and job contacts if you have them. Even if your loved one is housed in a different area, you might have access to the internet that he or she does not. So, it will be easier for you to find information about job listings in that area.

• *Home Confinement.* This is a release method as well as an alternative form of sentencing or a condition of bond. It involves a monitor placed around a person's ankle and a corresponding box plugged into the residential phone line which transmits information to the home-confinement officer or deputy. Usually the person being monitored is required to stay within a certain distance of the residence except for preapproved exceptions such as going to work, the grocery store, or the doctor. If the person is staying with you, what you will need to do is make sure you have a "land line" through the phone company. Because of the changes in technology over the years, issues often arise these days because the owner of the residence has transitioned from a home phone to a cell phone.

• ***Boot Camp.*** These programs use techniques developed by the military. They stress discipline, order, a scheduled life, personal achievement, physical prowess, and self-esteem. They encourage education and provide substance abuse services. They engender pride and encourage success. They are honest and don't play down a person's serious problems, but make an effort to seek ways around them. After such a program, people experience changes in attitude and are better equipped to begin their new lives.

It is important to remember that, whatever the program involved, not everyone succeeds. Some people break the rules, flee, or go back to using drugs and alcohol. When this happens, the person is sent back to the penitentiary to serve the rest of his or her sentence.

GUS'S STORY

The local jail's social service team received a call from Gus, who had been released two weeks earlier after a prison stay of several years. One of the team members asked how he was doing. Gus said he lived in a motel and had run out of money.

Gus had a serious drug problem. He also was classified as

mentally ill, occasionally believing himself to be some historical figure such as Napoleon. He wasn't physically aggressive, though. His usual crimes included theft, loitering, and other non-violent actions. He spent his jail and prison time in and out of the medical unit, depending on his current mental state.

After Gus hung up the phone, the social service team members attempted to find his family. They located his sister that same afternoon, but by the time they spoke to her, Gus already had been booked back into jail. He had stolen a neighbor's vehicle — the same one he stole the last time he was arrested — although he didn't have a driver's license. Every police officer in town knew him, so the arrest happened quickly.

Of course, he was charged again, convicted, and sent back to prison.

He later explained that he'd called the social service team to see if he still knew people that were part of it. He understood that they would pay attention to him and try to help him.

Like Gus, most inmates are excited and happy to get out of prison. They walk out through the gates and are filled with hope and good intentions. None of them leave with plans for ever returning. Like Gus, however, many lack the tools to survive and thrive on the outside. Most aren't as bad off as Gus, but still aren't ready to return immediately to independent living. Leaving prison, especially after many years, is a traumatic experience. Unlike Gus, whose personality and addictions made him rather docile, some folks dealing with the new world they find themselves in grow angry, frustrated, and even violent.

Prisons do try to prepare inmates for transition to the outside. Some facilities have programs that begin several months before release. There are classes to take, books to read, and videos to watch. The inmates are encouraged to make arrangements for housing, a job, and other immediate needs. They are advised to contact family and friends to establish a support network and find an initial place to stay. If that is not possible, prison counselors often will help the inmates find and contact halfway houses, SRO (Single Room Only) hotels, shared apartments, or other places that might be options for a newly freed person.

States vary as to what practical assistance they provide for inmates upon release. This might involve clothes, shoes, a bus or train ticket, or even a small amount of money. However, it also might be nothing at all except a ride to the bus or train station and a check the person can't cash for any money earned in prison or left on the trustee account. The days of providing freed prisoners with a horse and a twenty-dollar gold piece are in the past.

If your loved one is released with nothing, it would be helpful if you arrive on his or her release date and provide transportation. You will need to buy clothes, then remember to take them with you. If you can't pick up your loved one or can't afford clothes, your best bet is to contact the prison's chaplain. Often the chaplain will have donated clothing available for indigent inmates. The prison counselors also can offer advice on how to cash a prison release check or acquire a bus ticket if none has been provided.

Once people who have been released make it back to the cities where they live, they will have many other immediate needs. These include:

• *Food.* Day-to-day sustenance is important. However, most people leaving prison want something special for their first meal on the outside. Prison food is so bad that newly released prisoners often see that first meal as symbolic. If you can help with this, you will earn a lot of gratitude.

• *Clothing.* Many inmates leave prison with only the clothes they are wearing. If you've stored your loved one's old clothes and they still fit, that person is lucky.

• *Housing.* If a person is released on parole, initial housing already has been determined, whether with you or someone else. If not, help out however you can, but don't break the bank.

• *ID or Driver's License.* This can be one of the most complicated steps in getting a person back to a normal life. Because of current homeland-security concerns, getting a driver's license in most states requires two forms of identification (such as birth certificate and social security card), as well as proof of residence (which might include utility bills in a person's name). As someone newly released from prison, your loved one might have none of these. If so, you can assist that person to acquire the two forms of ID. The person likely will leave the facility with a prison ID card that can serve as one form, but these usually are valid only for 30 to 60 days. For the proof of residence, you (or whomever the person is living with) might have to go to the DMV office and sign a statement declaring that the person resides with you.

If your loved one was locked up for many years, he or she also likely will have to take a driver's test as if acquiring a license for the first time. If the person is borrowing your vehicle for the test, make sure that he or she knows all the ins and outs of the automobile, especially if it is a newer model. Features of cars might have changed significantly during the time your loved one has been away.

• *Job.* In some states, a person's parole officer will have a list of places that hire convicted felons. If this isn't true in your state, or if the person was released without parole, you can assist in the job search. Contact your friends and acquaintances to find out if any of them have positions available or know of places that are hiring. Check the newspapers and job websites such as Monster.com. Remember though that your loved one has to find and earn the job. All you can do is make suggestions and perhaps provide contacts.

• *Physical and Mental Healthcare.* If you can afford it, getting your loved one an appointment with your family doctor, county health department, or a local free (low-cost) clinic is a good place to start.

• *Substance Abuse Support.* Alcoholics Anonymous and Narcotics Anonymous will have meetings somewhere near wherever your loved one is staying. You can check the AA and NA websites to find out more information. Meetings also are listed in a city's daily newspaper.

• *Education, Job Training, or Mentoring.* Figure out what your loved one needs and is willing to do. Job skills classes provide valuable assistance. Participants learn how to seek jobs, write resumes, be successful at interviews, dress appropriately, and establish habits that enhance long-term job success.

• *Church Connections.* Not all released prisoners are particularly religious. For those that are, now is the time to get them started with a church, temple, mosque, etc. It can provide both a focus and an outlet for them as they readjust to society. In addition, other church members can be helpful in keeping your loved one on the right track.

VETERANS' PROGRAMS

Government services will be provided for veterans, even those that have been incarcerated. If your loved one has served in the military, it is important for him or her to seek out whatever programs are available and enroll as necessary.

In recent years, there has been an upsurge in diagnosis, understanding, and treatment of PTSD (*post-traumatic stress disorder*, formerly referred to as *combat fatigue* or *shellshock*). This malady develops after a person has been to war or suffered through other harsh and powerful events. It can cause that person to experience difficulties in dealing with everyday life, coping with stress, keeping a job, or forming stable relationships. It can cause someone to act irrationally, and in some cases might lead to delusions or hallucinations.

In the past, there was little information or support for people dealing with this condition. Now, however, more options exist. There are veterans' courts, for example, that provide mentoring and alternative sentencing with mental treatment for those suffering from PTSD that have been charged with crimes.

Not only is the government more proactive and realistic when dealing with veterans' issues, groups of veterans and concerned citizens have developed programs as well. Housing and other support services are provided in some areas. Drug and alcohol rehab programs are available that have been especially designed for veterans. Mentor programs and organizations that provide service animals are ready to assist. These groups can be located and researched easily on the internet.

For you, the important thing is to make the right people

aware of your loved one's status and any mental-health issues. The people that need to know include your loved one's lawyer in any ongoing criminal proceeding, the staff at medical or psychiatric units, and social workers or parole officers that might be in contact with the individual. By sharing this information, you can assure that these people will offer your friend or family member the appropriate level of care.

CHURCH GROUPS

The Rev. Will's church considers each person's situation individually. Sometimes a person can live with a parish family for a brief period of time. On occasion, the church or a member will help a person with rent for an inexpensive room. Folks from the congregation have provided furnished apartments or supplied food for families of those recently released from prison. They have tried to help people find jobs and have transported them to interviews. They encouraged participation in Alcoholic Anonymous or Narcotics Anonymous because these groups are aware of signs of stress that might lead to relapse, and they can provide that dimension of support.

What members of the church community hoped for was to empower the former prisoners and help them to rejoin society. However, Will and his congregation knew that this was short-term assistance. They didn't want to cause harm by allowing it to go on too long.

Will's hope was that the ex-cons and their families would become integral parts of the church community and then, in time, reach out to others as well.

Some churches and church-supported groups have

outreach programs such as Will's. These are designed for people who have been incarcerated. Ask at your church (temple, mosque, etc.). If such a program isn't available, church members might make suggestions or be able to find other ways to help your loved one.

THE LINGERING EFFECTS OF INCARCERATION

Myles was not mentally ill. He was a normal guy who had been incarcerated for several years. He said that he felt like everyone stared at him. He was apprehensive when riding on a bus or standing in a crowd. He spoke of feeling angry when someone at his halfway house changed the channel on the television in the recreation area. Myles thought he was going crazy. He hadn't given himself enough time for the transition back to living in the real world.

What factors of prison life cause these reactions? In prison, the inmates have very few choices. They are told when to get up and when to go to bed, when and what to eat, when to go outside, what to wear, etc. Daily decisions the average person makes (often without even stopping to consider them), prisoners have made for them by the facility staff.

In addition, prisoners are watched all the time, by the guards and other inmates. Correctional officers watch to make sure inmates are following the rules, but also for those inmates' own protection. Other prisoners watch out of fear for their own safety, to make sure no one is informing to the guards, and sometimes to find weaknesses on which they might prey or things they can steal. Everyone is observed. There is no privacy. Even the bathrooms are watchable in one way or another to prevent rapes or suicide attempts.

The sounds in prison impact a person's life. Doors clank at all hours. People shout and curse. Mentally ill individuals sometimes scream and make strange noises. There are echoes and reverberations through the long halls and open spaces. Inmates become alert to such sounds without realizing it. They also occasionally have long periods of total silence when locked in a single-person cell or restricted area.

Passing the time can be difficult, especially for those in segregation and those without jobs. Inmates grow accustomed to sitting, lying on their bunks, reading, watching television, playing cards, etc.

Even conversations are different on the inside. Other inmates might have different backgrounds, experiences, and ways of looking at the world that make understanding difficult. There is a jargon also that is spoken by prisoners. Special words have become standard replacements for more common ones. Vulgar phrases and street language are used. When a person returns to society and tries to interact with others or find work, these ways of thinking and speaking can cause problems.

Another thing you should be aware of when your loved one comes home is that much will have changed in the few years he or she has been away. While for you, these changes might have gone by in a slow progression so that you might not have noticed, for your loved one, they appear as one confusing jumble. Technology especially will seem so different as to be incomprehensible. Phones, computers, cars, and other electronic items all will have gone through several generations of upgrades. Helping your loved one understand all these changes will be an important step in his or her readjustment to freedom.

Finally, you might sense paranoia from your loved one, or at least a bit of mistrust. Try to understand that inmates often feel as if they are alone in a crowd. They learn quickly not to trust anyone. They keep important things to themselves so as not to be ridiculed. They keep their weaknesses secret so as not to be victimized. They look over their shoulders often and sit with their backs to the wall. This goes on for however many years they are prisoners. So, when they return home, how do they shift gears and act the way people on the outside do? Expect a period of adjustment and possibly even turmoil.

COMPLICATIONS

If your loved one, upon release, will be living with you, there are issues to consider. All who spend significant time incarcerated are impacted by their stay. Their trust level has changed. They might react to sounds you don't notice or be startled at sudden loud noises. They could find it difficult to make decisions. While they are glad to be out, they might experience depression or anxiety, especially when things like job searches or medical care move slowly. Worse, there is a good chance they will return to familiar hangouts, old friends, and negative behaviors. Try to be aware of what is happening in your loved one's life.

You also might have difficulties when your loved one returns, especially if you have a spouse or children living with you. Communication is crucial. You should talk with your spouse about changes and issues before the inmate is released. Even so, there will be surprises. Both of you will need to make adjustments. That is why communication is so important. You and your spouse can work on problems and solve them together.

Children in the home will have to adapt as well. Their reactions in the beginning might be positive, but if the returning loved one is their parent, as he or she reasserts power, the children could respond differently. Some kids will tell you straight out what they are thinking. Others might withdraw or act out. You should ask them, or have them draw a picture if they are too young to express themselves well enough verbally. You also might want to check with their teachers and counselors about any changes that might have been noticed at school. None of this is bad. It is just what happens when there are major changes to a stable situation. If these changes have a strong impact on a child, then counseling could prove necessary. Changes are difficult for people of any age, but children often suffer more because they don't understand or know how to describe what they feel.

As for the returning loved one, regardless of his or her relation to you or the rest of your family, you must establish rules to be followed before this person arrives. These include who does what chores, what belongs to whom, how much rent is owed and when it will be due, and how space may be utilized. Other smaller things should be considered as well: TV use, laundry times, kitchen cleanup, etc. These little details can be more problematic than the larger, more complicated issues and cause more tension in your household.

A weekly or monthly house meeting is a good idea. In the meeting, all members of the household can discuss how things are working and how problems can be fixed. Otherwise, conversations about such things will only occur when problems arise, which could lead to an argument rather than dialogue.

As stated before, you will want to keep an eye on your loved one. Because he or she has reverted to negative behavior in the past, you should state up front what you consider inappropriate behavior in your home and that any activities which are illegal or prohibited under terms of the person's parole will result in the person being asked to leave. This is important because any criminal activity (manufacturing meth, storing stolen goods, etc.,) could make you liable and therefore subject to lose your house, have your children taken away by social services, and ultimately result in *you* being charged with crimes. *This must be a clear and firm rule with no appeal for failure.*

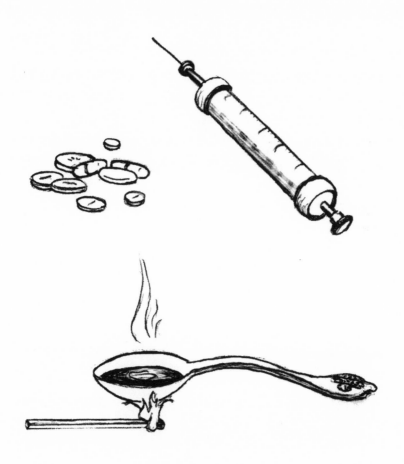

Part V.
Major Causes

DRUGS

GEORGIA WAS ONCE AN ORDINARY WIFE and mother. She kept a lovely house and had a good job. That was before she got involved with drugs.

A minor traffic accident resulted in an injury for which Georgia was prescribed painkillers. She liked the way she felt when she was on them and began taking more and more, often finding new excuses to go to the emergency room or schedule a visit with her doctor. The pills she took got stronger over time as well. Georgia soon became addicted and started buying her drugs illegally on the street.

Her marriage was destroyed. Her lifestyle changed completely. She stopped taking care of herself and was almost never at home.

Georgia was bright and could think clearly when not high. She found a good way to make money to buy the drugs. She became the leader of a salt and pepper team (people of color and whites working together) that shoplifted in all the malls in a four-state area. Georgia looked like a frumpy, white, middle-class housewife. Her team of young, mostly African-American friends stole goods from the stores in one mall, then went to another mall where Georgia returned the goods for cash. Georgia and her friends used the money to buy drugs. They were caught because one of her team was careless.

Most likely, Georgia returned to her life of crime when she left jail after a short stay. She was clever, and the police couldn't prove much.

There are many things that can lead a person to commit crimes. By far, the two most common are drugs and alcohol. If you do a survey in jails and prisons, you will find that over 66 percent of the inmates admit to having substance-abuse problems. In reality, that number is probably much closer to 90 percent. Incarcerated people try not to admit to problems that can extend their incarceration, and substance abuse is one of these. Even more are in denial about their addiction. They do not see the strong connection between drugs or alcohol and their illegal behavior.

No one ever sets out to be an alcoholic or a drug addict. Most folks firmly believe they can handle anything and stop whenever they want. They are lying to themselves as much as to everyone else. They are hooked and, in the majority of cases, can't quit on their own. Stopping drugs, alcohol, gambling, or any addiction is a life-long battle.

Different people start drinking or taking drugs for different reasons. It could be for relief from physical pain or psychological stress. It could be peer pressure and curiosity. In many cases, they grew up in a drug-abuse environment or with alcoholic parents. Sometimes, as with Georgia, it can be a complete accident. Many addicts report feeling as if a bomb went off in their heads when they first tried their drug of choice, so undoubtedly genetics plays some role. In any case, it could be a combination of the above or something else entirely. Why they started doesn't matter, except perhaps something they have to face in their recovery programs.

Often when people are arrested for the first time, they will deny any use of alcohol or drugs. They might say, "I tried it once," or, "It belongs to someone else," or even "Someone set me up," along with a hundred other possible excuses. They even deceive themselves into believing what they say to others.

They also try to minimize the size of the problem or the extent of their use. Many swear, "I only smoke a little weed." This often will be followed by their acknowledgment of having tried other illegal substances. Then they admit using one or more other drugs fairly regularly.

Some claim that because they go to work daily, they don't have a problem. Binge drinkers, for example, might drink only on weekends,. They fail to see the way this impacts their lives mentally and physically. If the disease takes over, they can lose everything, including their lives.

Families worry about their loved ones, and with good cause. Drinking and driving cause many auto accidents. Overdoses of street drugs are common, leaving people dead or impaired both mentally and physically. In addition, many young people take combinations of street and prescription drugs. This can lead to physical complications and even death. When pregnant women take drugs, they risk the lives and futures of their unborn children. Babies born to addicted mothers often have physical and mental problems.

If you think that isn't enough reason to worry, consider that both drugs and alcohol can lead to agitated states that generate fights and other forms of violence. The need for money to purchase drugs causes otherwise decent people to commit dangerous and illegal acts. These activities put them and others in harm's way.

Also, there are long-term effects of substance abuse. Alcoholics often have liver and other medical problems generated by their drinking. Those who sniff (huff) paint, glue, or other vapors damage brain cells and thus end up with decreased mental capacity. Certain drugs can lead to paranoia and mental illness. IV drug users face dangers of HIV/AIDS, hepatitis B, and other diseases. Meth destroys teeth and does other damage. Synthetic drugs often lead to new and unusual conditions as with the heroin substitute call krokadil (crocodile) that causes deadly infections. If that weren't enough, people caught up in their addictions tend to eat little and don't pay attention to nutrition. Nor do they worry about their hygiene.

Why give this list of potential problems? It's a warning. Inmates will tell their families, "This jail is terrible. I'm not safe, and I'm going crazy. Get me out and I'll never do it again." Then, when they hit the streets, they immediately go back to their old ways. If your loved one has been arrested, you should get that person out only if he or she will go into treatment. Remember, the addiction—the disease—and not your loved one is in control.

You also need to learn about addiction and the patterns that generate it. Go to Al-Anon meetings and get information from other family members of addicts and alcoholics. There are good books available, too. Being loyal to your loved one means attempting to understand what is going on, not just accepting everything he or she says at face value. Part of this disease is loss of control, and lying comes from that.

Ross was talking to the counselor about his alcohol problem. When asked how old he was when he began drinking, Ross answered that he was two. He said his father drank three quarters of a cup of Jack Daniel's in his breakfast coffee. Ross would climb on his father's lap and drink the coffee at that early age.

This is another hard thing to say. Unfortunately, sometimes the parents or siblings *get a person started* on drugs and alcohol. Or, family members and significant others *join in and become alcoholics or addicts themselves.*

Do you fit into one of those categories? Perhaps you even were aware of or took part in the same crime for which your friend or family member is now doing time. Just because your loved one got caught and you didn't, don't doubt that this is a serious issue for you. In stressful situations, do you turn to substances to solve your problems? *You might have a problem!* If you have even a slight suspicion that this is true, *get help now!*

Many people on the inside and often their partners on the outside are adult children of alcoholics. They don't know how to live a healthy lifestyle because their parents didn't model it. They grew up with unresolved feelings of deep hurt. Some children become the *responsible ones* and take care of others. Some are *invulnerable* and close themselves off from others. In addition, the *adjusters* are not in charge but fit into any situation, the *placaters* settle disputes and the *acting-out children* do just what the term implies.

Adult Children of Alcoholics programs, AA and Al-anon will have more information about these issues if this family system applies to you.

When asked if he had a substance-abuse problem, Floyd said, "I did, but not now."

"Great!" the counselor said. "How long had have you been clean and sober?"

Floyd responded, "Two months."

The next question was, "How long have you been in jail?"

The answer, as suspected was, "Two months."

The counselor laughed and said, "That's a crock! If you could get something, you wouldn't be clean and sober."

Floyd had detoxed—that is, he no longer had drugs in his system. Or, as the AA/NA folks would put it, he was clean, but he wasn't sober. He had changed neither his drug-user mindset nor his lifestyle. He had no support mechanism in place to make recovery a reality.

Your loved one might be able to get treatment as part of the sentence. Some correctional centers have drug treatment facilities. Also, sometimes the judge will order drug rehab as a condition of bond or probation. If a person really wants to stay sober, he or she should ask for help while still incarcerated. In most penitentiaries, there are AA/NA meetings even when no other programs are available. If these aren't the case or if treatment isn't available in prison, then *you* should do everything you can to ensure that your loved one seeks treatment at the time of his or her release.

There are rehab facilities and Alcoholics Anonymous/ Narcotics Anonymous meetings in almost every city in the United States. Look them up on the internet and urge your loved one to get help. As part of this, he or she will need to find a sponsor (a sort of guide for your loved one to talk to about any problems that arise and how to work the twelve steps), which can be accomplished simply by asking around at one of the meetings.

If your loved one is taking part in one of these programs, whether in prison or on the outside, it would be wise for you to attend Al-Anon, too. Al-Anon is the equivalent of AA/NA for family members of alcoholics and addicts. This group provides support, understanding, and guidance for people that might not otherwise know where to look. You need to be able to help your loved one both now and after release. If you understand what is going on, you can do so in the best possible way.

Maynard made his first visit to jail when he was a teenager. He returned many times. There were a few stretches in prison. He had many family members who also interacted regularly with the criminal justice system.

Maynard was in his thirties before he became willing to go into treatment. He was the first in his family to do so. He did well and was soon clean and sober.

However, his sobriety was short-lived. With some of his family and most of his friends still doing drugs, he relapsed and ended up back in jail for a time.

But this is a happy story. Maynard had the courage to go back into treatment. The second time he got sober, he stayed that way and began to build himself a new life.

When people go from incarceration back to the same setting as before their arrest or they surround themselves with the same bad influences, they will return to the same patterns. If they hang out with the same friends and go to the same taverns and parties, they will soon be back to the same old behaviors.

If your loved one returns to your home, you must consider the temptations he or she will face. You might decide to *remove alcohol from your home* (this could be a requirement if the person is on parole). You should at least consider it.

Sometimes a person tries to substitute a new drug for the old one that caused the problems. *Just a beer won't hurt*, says the recovering heroin addict. The truth is, when the addictive substance is removed, the person can become addicted to something else. Or, more likely, the person will feel this new drug isn't as pleasing, and so he or she will return to the old one.

Even after stopping drugs, some people experience unclear thinking, inability to concentrate and/or memory problems. Inappropriate emotional responses such as mood swings, overreactions, and difficulties handling stress often occur. Sleep problems, bad dreams, and even physical coordination troubles can develop. These are common among recovering addicts and alcoholics. It often takes six months to a year for a person just to feel normal again. Rehab counselors also like to point out that people stop aging emotionally when they become addicts or alcoholics. If your loved one started drinking at fifteen and gets sober at forty-five, he or she might still have the emotions of a fifteen-year-old. So, be patient.

Those of you who know someone who is addicted have seen a progressive change in that person. The wonderful, lovable, friendly, playful, loyal, trustworthy individual you knew seems to have disappeared. Now this person is preoccupied, loses control, makes excuses, shows resentment, and displays aggressive behavior. Along the way, you have witnessed fear, confusion, and withdrawal. Family problems arise. There are issues at work and school. Then the police come knocking. This is the rule, not the exception.

One of the biggest problems with personality changes due to addiction is the lack of control that leads to lying. When deeply involved in the addiction scene, it becomes easier and more comfortable to lie. Before long, an addict can't distinguish what is true and what is false, what is real and what is imaginary. Moral standards have disappeared. Illegal and unethical actions are rarely given a second thought. The addict's friends also have this attitude.

People caught in the addiction cycle seek quick remedies for the experience of pain. They make poor choices because they believe this temporary relief will help. The temporary relief distorts reality but backfires when the pain returns. This requires continued denial, and the guilt and shame bring a feeling of complete hopelessness.

Looking back, undoubtedly you understand what was happening. You might have seen the problem but not labeled it. Maybe you did know but couldn't believe it. Don't spend your time worrying about what might have been. Deal with what is happening in the present.

There is hope for your loved one's recovery. An *intervention* is one way to convince an addict to begin treatment. An addiction professional leads significant people in the addict's life as they explain how that person's substance abuse affects them. They tell the addict what they have seen in his or her behavior, share their concern for the addict's wellbeing, and their intention to no longer enable such destructive behavior (that is, to help the addict by providing money, covering for negative actions, failing to speak out, etc.). These people then urge the addict to seek treatment.

Before your loved one can change, however, he or she has to *want* to change. Alcoholism is a disease. Addiction is a disease. Medical help might be required, as will new ways of thinking and new attitudes. There are twelve-step programs, addiction centers offering group therapy, support groups, and counselors. It took a long time for your loved one to reach this point, and it will take a long time for things to seem normal again. Your loved one will face many difficulties: getting a job, returning to a scheduled life, relating to people, etc. Relapse might even be a part of the experience.

Recovery is a long process. Be there to offer support.

GAMBLING

Pierce had a small, profitable home repair business. He was well known and respected because he did good work and charged reasonable rates. Friends recommended Pierce's company to other friends.

Several new forms of legal gambling popped up in the area. Pierce tried the slot machines first, just for fun, and then moved on to blackjack. After he started to gamble, he couldn't stop.

Pierce came to jail with fraud charges. He would make new contracts at work, take payment for materials, and then gamble with the money and lose. Then he wouldn't go back and finish the jobs for which he had been paid. Instead, he would take new jobs and do the same thing again. This behavior caught up with him quickly, as did the police.

Gambling has been around for a long time. Even in the Bible there are stories of casting lots and other games of chance. Undoubtedly, the addiction of gambling is that old. In recent years, gambling problems in our country have increased due to legalization and easy access to gaming facilities as well as online sites that offer sports betting and poker.

What has been said about other forms of addiction is true

for gambling. However, in one way, gambling can be worse. When a person has sobered up from drugs or alcohol, he or she can begin life again, but a gambler still must deal with debts incurred because of the addiction.

Gambling addiction is a progressive disorder just like taking drugs. Betting increases, and larger amounts of money are needed to get the same excitement. The gambler wants to win again and again, as well as to recover from losses. Compulsive gamblers forget to eat, sleep, and care for bodily functions. They skip work. They gamble to make money, then borrow money to finance gambling. They often turn to illegal measures to fund their gambling habit.

If your loved one has a gambling problem, the first thing you should do is check all your assets. You might find that savings accounts, stocks, insurance policies, retirement funds, and other financial resources are gone. Old and new credit cards could be maxed out. You might discover that the house is mortgaged, has a second mortgage, has liens against it, or even worse. Bills will likely not have been paid, and penalties are growing. Check things like taxes that, if left unpaid, could burden you for years and perhaps result in federal charges being filed against *you*. Even check your valuables such as jewelry, antiques, and electronics that easily can be pawned.

In addition, money might have been borrowed, either in the usual way or from loan sharks at high rates. This could even be a safety issue. Find out as much as you can from your loved one and be prepared for the worst possibilities.

You will need both legal and financial assistance to get this mess straightened out. Don't let the problem remain in the hands of the gambler. Your loved one still might not be facing up to this problem. Act fast, show an honest effort, and hopefully creditors will agree to wait.

Men and women, young and old, develop gambling addictions. Even children and teens get involved in things like the lottery, sports betting, fantasy sports, and now internet games. They are not supposed to be able to participate, but unauthorized games exist. It isn't difficult to slip by the regulations.

There are several types of gamblers:

• *Professional Gamblers.* These people make their living by gambling. They tend to be controlled and smart. They often have been playing for years. They know the ropes and make their money not by "beating the house" but by taking it from other less-experienced gamblers.

• *The Anti-social Gambler.* This person gets money by illegal activities such as fixing games, point shaving, horse doping, etc.

• *The Casual Social Gambler.* These folks gamble once in a while but never allow their gambling patterns to escalate.

• *The Serious Social Gambler.* This person gambles regularly but usually doesn't escalate to addictive levels unless stress arises.

• *The Relief and Escape Gambler.* For these people, gambling is a major activity. They can stop unless a major stress enters their life. Many frequent gamblers not yet at the addiction level fall under this category. They often can be spotted sitting at poker machines in bars or buying an above-average number of lottery tickets at the convenience store.

• *The Compulsive Gambler.* Compulsive gamblers are the ones for whom gambling is the only thing in life that matters. They cannot stop without help.

Gambling is an emotional issue. Some gamblers have

preferred games and venues. Others enjoy betting on anything. There are casinos, horse and greyhound racetracks, sports books, fantasy sports leagues, card games, lotteries, bingo halls, community or church raffles, and many other ways a person can be tempted. It is easy to get hooked.

If your loved one has a problem, he or she needs help before it becomes too late. There are special hotlines and Gamblers Anonymous (GA) meetings. There are financial counselors that work with gamblers to get their money situations in order. Casinos and other gambling establishments have elimination programs and refuse entrance to those that self-identify as gambling addicts. Some states have passed laws that prevent those in financial difficulty from gambling or entering places where gambling occurs.

You might be gambling with your loved one. For you, it is recreational, and so it might take you a long time to recognize your loved one's problem. At that point, you feel betrayed. If so, remember that your loved one probably couldn't help it. Gambling, as with drugs, is a disease that effects rational decision-making. Get help for yourself, get help for your loved one, and remember that you are not alone. Seek professional assistance in the legal and financial areas before it is too late. Encourage your loved one to seek help. *Take control over your finances.*

OTHER FORMS OF ADDICTION

There are other forms of addiction, eating and sex chief among them. The patterns for these addictions are similar to those for drugs, alcohol, and gambling. While such addictions are less likely to lead to your loved one's arrest, you should watch for signs of compulsive behavior anyway, because extremes are often dangerous.

In some cases—quitting cigarettes, for example—a person might trade the nicotine habit for another addiction, perhaps a psychological one like compulsive eating. Any addiction can cause problems for your loved one's health or instability in your home. Sex addiction, especially, can take a person to some rather dark places and might result in the police getting involved (soliciting a prostitute, for example).

Help is out there. There are twelve-step programs for most forms of addiction. Others understand what you are going through. They have been there and often can suggest positive things you can try to make the situation better. You need to talk to someone. Remember, people do recover and put their lives back together. There is always hope.

FEAR

The dictionary says fear is a painful emotion marked by alarm, dread, disquiet, anxiety, panic, terror, fright, apprehension, horror, etc. All people experience fear at some point in their lives. Likewise, they have their own circumstances that cause it.

Human beings experience this chemically inside their bodies by adrenaline rush and the fight-or-flight instinct that pops up in uncomfortable or dangerous situations. Often fear comes from negative past experiences. Other times, people become aware in a more general sense of possible dangers ahead. Even so, some fears are irrational because they involve things that are dangerous only in a person's mind. These fears can develop into phobias (coulrophobia, for example, is the irrational fear of clowns) and anxieties (social anxiety might leave a person feeling paralyzed around others).

People react to fear differently in different situations. Some flee, scream, or even faint. Some become quiet or do anything to avoid situations that might frighten them. Sometimes the reaction might resemble another emotion such as anger.

If your loved one develops phobias or anxieties, urge him or her to seek help. Some psychiatrists specialize in treating these sorts of things and, if the condition is a chemical one, there are medications that might make a person feel normal.

Often, all you can do is be supportive of former inmates facing fear. People who have been in jail or prison might be good at hiding their fear because they have had so much practice. On the outside, they might be concerned about their safety because they trained themselves that way while they were behind bars. They might lock doors and windows, pull shades, stay inside.

Be gentle and sensitive when a person is demonstrating fear. Always remember that your reasons and reactions are probably different from theirs.

At the same time, it is important that you guide your loved one into some form of treatment for his or her fear. Fear can be a factor leading to substance abuse or even crime. When people come to a fork in the road, they have a tendency to choose the easier path. If, however, they are afraid (even irrationally) of the easier path, the more dangerous one might seem easier to them. If a man, for example, is afraid of telling his wife that he has a gambling problem, he might find it easier to commit a robbery for money than to say those few simple words.

Fear for the person on the outside can revolve around a parent's or spouse's concern for the safety and wellbeing of the person inside. They might fear that relatives and friends will not accept the person. They might be afraid of going to visit the inmate, either because of the prison itself or the people encountered there. They also might fear that they are bearing the stigma that goes with the incarcerated person as though being blamed for their loved one's actions. Finally, when the person is released, they might worry about his or her return to the family.

All people have their own sets of fears. Whatever yours are, if they get out of hand or control your life, counseling could be necessary.

THE OTHER SECRET

Eugene's life of crime began with stealing clothes and shoes from back yards and porches. Then he started breaking into homes to steal these items, especially the shoes. Eventually he attacked women on the street. According to the newspapers, he would knock a woman down, steal her shoes, and then lick her feet.

Eugene was caught, arrested, and put in jail. He was tried on several charges, convicted, and sentenced to a long prison term. The judge ran his sentence consecutively (each sentence starting only after the previous sentence ends) rather than concurrently (all sentences running at the same time).

Eugene was bewildered that he had over a hundred years to serve just for stealing shoes. He asked why he got a sentence that was longer than some murders and was told that the fear he created in the community was the most likely reason. The judge also was concerned because Eugene's crimes became more and more aggressive. He had moved from petty theft to residential burglary, and then to physical attacks.

Eugene was sent to prison. About a year later, he returned to jail for a resentencing. He had won an appeal, so his sentence was shortened somewhat.

While in prison, he received counseling in a sex offender program. He spoke to his counselor about 'paraphilia.' That was the term he used. Paraphilia means recurrent intensive sexual urges lasting six months or more involving non-consenting people. He had begun to understand that his behavior was sexual in nature, and therefore a serious problem.

If your loved one is charged with a sex-related crime, it is difficult to bear. Because sex charges are violent and betray another person, they also can be difficult to understand. Society finds it easier to condemn this kind of crime. Even other criminals in prison often think of sex offenders as monsters and will attack them just because of their charges.

There is another side to this. You know your loved one and believe he or she is not guilty. In some cases, it is one person's word against another's. These days, however, DNA testing has taken at least some of the subjectivity from crime evidence and testimony. As such, many families will have to face the fact that their loved one has indeed committed a serious sex crime.

People who commit these crimes are out of control. Something in their heads (perhaps a history of abuse from their own childhoods or perhaps something more subtle) causes them to seek out and indulge in this aberrant behavior. Whatever the reason, they need counseling—for a long time, possibly the rest of their lives.

If your loved one has a problem like this, it might be difficult for you to accept. Even if you don't believe it, however, you must encourage him or her to get treatment. You do not want to see further hurt and damage to your loved one or the potential victims of any future crimes.

You, too, will benefit from counseling. The impact of this situation creates disruption in your life. Counselors can help you return quickly to normalcy.

There are a few support groups for you as you deal with your loved one's problem. The National Association for the Mentally Ill (NAMI) is established in many areas. You might also go to Al-Anon meetings. Others in these groups have been through difficult times themselves. It helps to listen to the balance others have reached as you seek your own. Even small similarities can offer options you have not yet considered. You also might look for a person who can help you on a one-to-one basis.

The more you know about this problem, the better you will be able to help your loved one. You need to understand the characteristics of the problem and how to identify the signs that relapse might occur. Even a single appointment with a counselor or social worker can give you insights. Share everything with your counselor and ask how to deal with specific problems.

Don't stop there. The library and internet both have information on your loved one's problem. The resource librarian at your local library can help you.

Eugene's experience shows that understanding is just the first step to containing the problem. Sexual disorders are partly addictions and partly mental illnesses. Like other addictions and mental problems, they will involve life-long struggles and a lot of help. Almost no one recovers from these illnesses alone. Your loved one needs counseling. Without it, there is little hope for change

The use of alcohol or drugs also impacts sex-related crimes. Different drugs have specific effects, such as stimulation, depression, or euphoria, which can lower the sense of responsibility and stimulate the sexual drive. If your loved one has been accused of a sex crime, do whatever it takes to keep him or her away from intoxicating substances.

Sentences for sex crimes are long because they generate fear and cause great personal violation. In some cases, as in Eugene's, there will be several incidents and escalation in the type of crime. If the person isn't caught right away, more serious crimes are likely to occur, possibly progressing to physical harm and murder, and then even longer sentences.

Some sex offenders commit crimes of opportunity — that is, if they are alone with the victim, they take advantage. Others actively seek victims. Some people only commit specific types of crime. They prefer a particular sex, age, body-type or other characteristic. Eugene's case is an example. At first, he didn't do anything other than steal clothes and shoes, which gave him some sort of sexual arousal, unusual as it is. There are others who commit different types of sex crimes, though this is rare, because part of the illness usually involves developing a pattern.

Many sex crimes are never reported. The crime with which your loved one has been charged might not have been the first committed. Some perpetrators have many victims before being caught and arrested.

In some states, treatment in prison is mandated for all those convicted of sex crimes. Release will be dependent on the decisions of doctors and other professionals in this unit. These decisions are based on how dangerous the person is to the community. If professionals decide offenders are a threat to others, these inmates will not be released and instead will be kept in a mental facility following a civil court action (Civil Placement). Regular evaluations are made and progress tracked so that when no danger to the community exists, the person can be released.

Those convicted of sex crimes must register with local police when they leave prison as well as any time they change addresses, and they must renew that registration once or twice a year, depending on the rules of that jurisdiction, laws of the state and the type of crime. Sex-offender registration provides information to police, schools, employers, neighbors, and other interested parties. If a person does not register he or she will be arrested, put in jail, fined, and possibly returned to prison. Failure to register is a new crime in itself.

ABUSE OF CHILDREN

Randolph was convicted of molesting many boys in a scheme that involved taking the children to summer camp. He was arrested, tried, and convicted.

When asked about the things he had done and the children he had harmed, he said, "I was only educating them."

If your loved one is accused of pedophilia—a sex crime involving children—this generates additional considerations.

If you have children in the home, your loved one should not return home until all people living there have had counseling. Your children's counselors and your loved one's counselor must permit such a move. *Your highest concern must be for the safety and wellbeing of your children.*

Sex offenders often have specific restrictions placed on them by the courts or state statutes. They must register and give the required information. They must live a specific distance from schools. They are not allowed on or near school grounds, children's parks, and other places where children congregate. They may not be employed as teachers, coaches, counselors, school bus drivers, religious youth mentors, etc.

Your loved one might have difficulty following these rules, or even admitting to a problem. Denial and minimization are common among sex offenders. They do this so they can live with themselves. They lie and deny again and again. Many sex offenders have been abused themselves and have developed layers of self-protection that must be broken down by a therapist. Because of this, treatment takes a long time.

For many pedophiles, part of the process and excitement is grooming the victim—that is, slowly finding methods of control. They try to desensitize the child to sex and then manipulate the child to keep the secret. For this reason, many of these individuals know how to be pleasant. They become a "friend" and gain not only the child's trust but that of the child's relatives and guardians as well. In extreme cases, pedophiles have been known to marry people with children of the age and style they seek.

It is important for you to understand that *all* children in a home where abuse occurs need counseling, even if they were not victims. Parents and other adults around the child need counseling and information, too. This information includes how to help the child recover, heal, and learn normal behaviors.

If nothing is done for the children, this experience will have a negative influence on the rest of their lives. It could stunt their normal psychological development leaving them child-like. It might lead to substance abuse to cover the pain. It can induce behavioral problems, isolation, inward turning, and a fear of others. It might have a negative impact on their sex life later on. Such children might even become perpetrators themselves. *Get the children help.*

Furthermore, protection of children must be your highest priority. You might have to deny your loved one some forms of support to ensure the safety of the children. This could mean making alterative housing arrangements so that this person will only be able to visit at scheduled times when someone can be there to observe. You must never allow a perpetrator to be alone with the children.

Your loved one's presence at family celebrations must be regulated if the victim or other children will be present. Possible psychological damage to the victim should be factored into your decision making. This can be difficult for you.

Remember, no matter what your loved one *says,* actions are what you must watch. A person might believe it when saying that he or she doesn't want to sexually abuse kids anymore, but even so, given an opportunity, the temptation might prove too great.

When a pedophile is tempted and close to relapse, there are signs that should be visible if you are paying attention. Increasing frustration, resentment, and hostility are a few of the more common ones. Withdrawing from others can signal a dangerous turn in your loved one's condition. Agitation or a negative mood also should be noticeable. One red flag is a problem with drugs and alcohol. Returning to activities that allow the person access to potential victims is the most serious. Watch out for these things, and keep your loved one's counselors informed.

Finally, you need to prepare yourself for external social pressures that might develop because of your loved one's crime. You might experience the negative reactions of friends, neighbors, and others. If you take a convicted sex offender back into your home, you might experience backlash from people in your community. These reactions come from fear and lack of understanding. If you do not feel strong enough to cope, other arrangements should be made. Your loved one might need to move to another area. If so, make sure he or she follows through with sex-offender registration, counseling, and other types of treatment.

MENTAL HEALTH

Garrick was diagnosed as bipolar (manic depressive). He had lived with his aunt only a few weeks after being released from a mental institution.

Garrick's disorder was characterized by extremes of high and low moods that sometimes left him too depressed to get out of bed in the morning, while at other times so manic he almost believed he could fly. He was supposed to be on medication to keep these problems under control, but he stopped taking his pills and began using street drugs.

One day, Garrick came home high on cocaine and demanded the keys to his aunt's car. When she refused, he grew enraged and struck out, killing her. He was arrested and charged with murder.

After his arrest, Garrick was first sent to a secure mental-health facility. When he finally made it to jail, he was disconnected and confused, not to mention highly medicated. He walked slowly, talked in a mumble, and was unable to communicate beyond a few simple words.

Jake, another inmate in the medical unit began to talk to him. Jake helped Garrick establish some balance, pointed out faulty thinking, and encouraged clear views.

Jake was in the medical unit because of a serious physical illness. He was middle-aged and had spent a number of years in prison. An intelligent, knowledgeable person, he had attended good schools and continued to take courses during his years in prison. He was also a keen observer of people. He decided to help because he and Garrick were the two that stayed for the longest period in that small medical unit. He said that he knew he would die soon and was making his own peace with God.

Slowly, Garrick began to return to rationality. His talks with Jake were the keys that facilitated changes in his mental state. His medication also was adjusted. Eventually he became stable enough to enter the general population. He took classes and passed his GED with a credible score. He began to write poetry and essays. He became a worker in the laundry.

Because of his crime, Garrick did go to prison. Even so, he managed to keep his illness under control despite the difficult setting.

About a third of the people who are incarcerated suffer from some form of mental illness, whether diagnosed or not. In many cases, like Garrick, they can regulate their actions with medication, an understanding of the disease, and the support of friends.

If your loved one has a history of mental illness, it likely is one of the factors leading to his or her incarceration. Even so, keep in mind that mental illness in all likelihood is not the only factor. Crimes committed solely because of mental illness are infrequent, and most mentally ill people never do anything illegal or get arrested.

You might want to inform the medical unit at the jail. It will alert them to watch for symptoms. If your loved one should be on drugs for a mental condition and doesn't take them, let the jail's medical staff members know so they can provide the correct medications and make sure these are taken. Most jails only continue the medications a person is prescribed before incarceration. New medications require new prescriptions from the jail doctor.

Often people prescribed psychotropic drugs (medication designed to alter a person's mental state or mood) don't like to take them. They experience side effects and unpleasant reactions to some medications. Most doctors will try to prescribe drugs that control the mental disorder but have the least severe side effects. Institutions, on the other hand, sometimes give people the least expensive drugs of the type needed. This can lead to different side effects and cause new problems for the people taking the medication. Speak to your loved one to see if this has happened and find out about any new side effects he or she experiences.

Unfortunately, some people stop taking prescribed medications and turn to street drugs to solve their problems. This is dangerous. Your loved one might feel good, but the controls on behavior are absent.

Norbert asked a counselor for help because "the people" were bothering him. When the counselor went to see him in his cell in the medical unit, she talked to him about getting along with others for the brief time he would be in jail. She thought she was getting through to him and that he understood. Then she asked which of the other inmates created the problem. He said they were little green men, and one of them was over there sitting on the windowsill. Fortunately, Norbert was already in the medical unit, and the staff knew about his problems.

The experience with Norbert shows that the more you know about a situation, the more helpful you can be. When people are delusional, their reality is distorted. If your loved one sees things that are not there or hears voices that others don't, this can be a sign of schizophrenia, dementia, or several other disorders involving flawed brain chemistry. These disorders can lead to violent outbursts, so should not be taken lightly. At the same time, they aren't your loved one's fault. He or she suffers from a disease which, as with all diseases, requires treatment. Seek out professional help from a qualified psychiatrist.

If your mentally ill loved one wants to return to your home, be sure you are safe. If the person is aggressive or violent toward you, find another place for that person to live. *Don't bring a violent person who has injured you back into your home.* This will not help you or your loved one, and it could result in injury to you. It is too easy for a mentally-ill person to slip back into the negative patterns that lead to violence. This is dangerous for you, for others in your home, even others in your neighborhood. This is a safety issue, not a love issue. Though it might seem like a harsh thing to say, *your loved one has done this before and will do it again.* Believe that until you see proof to the contrary.

Get to know the symptoms of your loved one's illness. You can go to the library, check the internet, ask the doctor, go to your local association for the mentally ill (NAMI)), contact the social worker, etc. It also could prove useful for you to talk to someone else who helps a person suffering from mental illness.

As with so many other things, having a relative with mental illness can be a secret of the family. Don't let this prevent you from getting help. Keep learning as much as you can about this illness. Don't let this illness destroy your life and peace of mind. You might not be able to "fix" your loved one, but you can gain a better understanding and receive support.

There are other things you can do. For example, keep alert for new medications, treatments and programs that also might improve the quality of your loved one's life. If you are a parent and getting older, assist your son or daughter to find others that can offer psychological support and assistance when you no longer are able to do so. Still, even if all you can do is offer love to your mentally-ill friend or family member, do that. Sharing and caring are most important. Sometimes just being there is enough, even when no practical things seem to make a difference.

No matter what, remember that you are not alone. Many others have mentally-ill friends and family members. If they can make it through this, so can you.

Part VI.
Choices for You

DOING TIME ON THE OUTSIDE

MANY FAMILIES ARE ALMOST RELIEVED when a person who has a dangerous lifestyle is arrested and is in jail or prison. At least they know where they are and that they are "safe." People who end up "in the system" regularly tend to be substance abusers or mentally ill. Their loved ones have tried everything and have been unsuccessful in helping them. Once people interact with the criminal justice system, their family and friends come under new pressure, both internally and externally, to help them. They are *doing time on the outside*.

Probably the fact that your loved one is in jail is not a surprise. Family members can be aware of the lifestyle this person is leading but are powerless to change it. Frequently it is the end of a downward spiral of difficulties and the continuation of a pattern of confrontation with the law. That does not make this any easier for you. It doesn't lessen the fear you feel for your loved one. It makes your anger more real. It brings your emotions to the forefront when you realize the great impact that your loved one's negative patterns are having on you and those around you. Each person's reaction is unique and their emotions are their own.

These patterns are common. You are not alone. Others

have experienced this, too. Always remember, emotions are neither right nor wrong, good nor bad. What you do because of these emotions, on the other hand, are choices and will be positive or negative. Your actions can help or hinder you and your loved one. Look at the emotions you experience and see how they affect your actions. Only you can analyze a situation and decide how to proceed.

This section of the book is designed to help you understand some of the choices you will encounter and suggest ways to deal with them. It is about how this new reality will affect you, as well as steps you can take to restore some normalcy in your life.

THE CHILDREN

Forest and Eva are in their late sixties. They run a business together. Eva is the office manager/bookkeeper, and Forest is the production and transportation expert. They are almost ready for retirement.

Their son and daughter-in-law are both facing long-term incarceration on drug charges, leaving behind two children and no family other than Forest and Eva to take care of them.

Should Forest and Eva take the kids? They know this decision will impact them for the next fifteen or twenty years. They realize that raising children puts demands on people of any age.

Although they are in a satisfactory financial situation, the couple will spend a lot of money to care for these children. Eva will leave her membership in the local historical preservation society. Forest will take additional responsibility for the business and won't be able to do much fishing or hunting. Many of the activities the two

*enjoy together will go by the wayside because one of them will have
to be with the children most of the time.*

*Forest and Eva, if their health holds, will do a good job raising the
kids. They will, however, face much frustration, many difficulties,
and a long rugged road before these young ones are on their own.*

Providing care for children is an immediate concern.
If you are asked to take care of your loved one's kids, you
have a serious decision to make. Whether you can handle
this responsibility throughout the entire process or only for
a few days, you must look realistically at your own health,
age, and ability to adjust to changes in your life. How great a
disruption will this be? Can you and your spouse do this? If
you believe you can, then do so.

If it isn't possible, then help the parent make other
arrangements. Don't feel guilty. If you can't do something
well, then making other arrangements is the best solution.
Visit the children regularly, be supportive, and continue your
relationship with them.

If the custodial parent is arrested, in most cases the other
parent will care for the children. If the other parent isn't able
to do so, can the grandparents take over? Is there an uncle or a
cousin that would be willing? Will arrangements be short- or
long-term? How will this impact the children?

No matter what happens in the short term, the people
caring for the children require a document giving them
temporary custody so that these kids can get medical
treatment if needed and also register to attend school. This can
be a simple statement signed by the custodial parent that will
need to be notarized. Most prisons have employees licensed
as notaries, but jails might not. So, arrangements with your

loved one's lawyer must be made. The beginning and ending date (e.g. during incarceration or until released from jail, etc.) should be included.

If no one in the immediate area can care for the children the local DCFS (Department of Children and Family Services) or its equivalent in your state will take temporary responsibility. This means that if you have to travel to get the kids, they will be cared for until you arrive. It also might be that the kids stay in state care until the case is settled or the parent released.

If there is no one to care for the kids and the incarceration will be long-term, then permanent placement and even adoption might have to be considered. Each state has its own laws about this subject, but usually a judge must be involved in the decision-making process. Family Court judges specialize in determining the best interests of children.

Whatever happens, it is important that the incarcerated person be informed and consulted.

It might be necessary for the children to receive counseling during this trying time. If you have the children, let the school counselor know the situation so that the school staff will be attentive, observe behavior, and understand problems that arise. Young people often act out in frustration rather than talk about their issues.

Another decision involves what to tell the children. Honesty is important. *Don't lie.* Lies always come back to haunt you. You might choose not to tell every fact or detail, but offer as much truth as you think they can handle.

Explanations will be an ongoing thing. If the child visits or talks to the parent on the phone, additional questions can arise. If the situation is long term, ongoing reports to the child about what is happening might help. You will want the child to interact with the parent by writing, drawing pictures, telling stories, and so on.

It is always wise to keep the child's view of the parent as positive as possible. You might be angry, but don't add to a child's confusion and frustration by painting the parent in a negative light. This child might return to the parent's custody in the future. The success of this child's life with the parent depends on your discretion now. If you must speak of the crime, explain as gently as you can that good people sometimes do bad things. Everyone makes mistakes once in a while.

OTHER CONCERNS

There are other practical things that, if applicable, demand immediate attention:

• *Pets.* Animals need care. If your loved one has a pet, can you or another family member take it? Another option is to leave the animals in their current location with someone regularly bringing food and water, as well as meeting other needs. That extends time to find temporary or permanent placement. If a good home can't be found and no one can care for it otherwise, the pet must be turned over to an animal shelter. However, remember that pets are like a member of the family. Your loved one might feel sadness and possibly anger at its loss.

• *Cars.* Vehicles are another issue. If your loved one's car has been impounded, the cost grows daily, so it would be wise to get it out of impound as soon as possible. If it is not worth the cost or the time impounded has been too long, your loved one might decide to let the jurisdiction sell the car. If that is the case, retrieve your loved one's personal property from the vehicle. Call the impound lot and determine the process and paperwork needed.

If not impounded, the vehicle still should be located and driven to a safe place. After a time, if a car is left parked on the street or in a business or private lot, it will be towed. Moving the vehicle to an acceptable parking location is a kindness.

In addition, if your loved one's incarceration will be long, there are taxes to be paid and state inspections to make sure the vehicle is roadworthy. Driving the vehicle at least once a week should keep parts from becoming faulty due to underuse. Things like tires and batteries often go bad if the car is parked too long.

Lastly, the car might have to be sold to pay for legal fees or any of your loved one's debts. Discuss this with him or her first. Selling the vehicle might require a notarized power of attorney signed by him or her.

• *Housing.* People often lose their houses or apartments while incarcerated because they aren't able to pay the rent, mortgage, taxes, etc. If you can afford it, paying for these things would be a great gift. If your loved one will be gone a long time or if you don't have the funds, at least collect the person's belongings. These will be dumped in the street if no one takes responsibility for them. It is so much easier to start again for people that have their basic items like clothes and furniture.

• *Immediate Business.* Your person needs someone trustworthy to handle ongoing everyday things. This could encompass anything from paying credit card bills to returning borrowed items. It also might mean something more intensive such as taking over management of your loved one's shop. You need to decide if you will do all these tasks. If you know you can't or won't, then tell your loved one immediately so he or she can make other arrangements. *Never say you will do something unless you can and will.* If you are unsure, say you will try.

THINGS TO REMEMBER

• *You Deserve Respect.* You should do everything you can to help your loved one. The problem is that some people get so involved with using negative behavior and manipulation that they do and say almost anything to get what they want. Inmates and substance abusers have been known to change the truth or see things only from their point of view. They do this to gain some benefit. Perhaps they are frantic. Over and over, they demand that family members contact their lawyer. They beg or even demand money the family does not have. They ask their families to do inappropriate things such as smuggle in drugs or tobacco without a second thought that this might be illegal. Don't let your loved one take advantage of you or talk down to you. You deserve respect, and you must not allow anyone to treat you like you are the bad guy.

• *You Need Balance.* Don't act immediately. Give yourself time to reflect before you decide what to do. Work against feelings of guilt. Know that you are okay.

• *Your Loved One Has Not Told You The Whole Story.* You are special to your loved one. People don't want those special in their lives to know the negative things they have done or experienced. They want to feel good about themselves and want you to think well of them also. They don't share the bad stuff. In many ways, this is not lying, but a self-protective cover. It might even be better for you if you don't know all the details. You would be fearful all the time if you knew the danger. Most of us don't share the real serious stuff with anyone.

• *Some Things That Happen To You During Your Loved One's Incarceration Are Unfair.* You might be treated poorly by the institutions, the criminal justice system, the prison system, or other individuals. You did not commit a crime, yet here you are, going through metal detectors, being searched, and not being trusted. You end up waiting for long periods of time. You ask questions and get no answers. Most people have no idea how cruel the system can be. It is a good idea for you to consult with someone else who understands the system. You might want to call the chaplain or a social worker to learn more. Above all else, be patient. No matter what happens, no matter what injustices you feel, don't lose your cool.

• *Help Is Available For You, Too.* There are support groups for families of inmates. Al-Anon meetings might help. Kairos Outside is a retreat weekend for women with incarcerated relatives. There are organizations that work to protect inmates and others that seek to change and improve the system. *You are not alone.*

SUMMARY OF ACTIONS AND ATTITUDES FOR NOW AND THE LONG HAUL

• *Be There.* Most of the actions you take will not be new or unique. Still, you might be the only lifeline for your loved one as well as a real agent of balance and normalcy in his or her life. The most important thing you can do is be there. Even if you don't have money or other forms of assistance to offer, that you are there so he or she doesn't feel alone is a valuable gift.

• *Be a Listening Ear.* The easiest and most frequently used lifeline is the telephone. It also might be the most expensive and least convenient method of communication. If your financial situation is strong, unlimited calls can be accepted. If your finances are limited, set up a schedule for calls. Be sure to use your telephone time in an efficient way. Make a list in a convenient place of essential information and special comments and stories to be shared. Keep your loved one informed about family and friends. Provide business information such as financial successes and failures, purchases, cost of items, etc. However, don't let your calls be all information and business. Save a little time to share words of hope, love, and sympathy. Be guided by the reactions of your loved one. There might not be much to say at times, but that is okay, too. Just be prepared to listen and share.

Don't feel you need to let every call go on and on as a gripe session. If your loved one becomes angry, starts using foul language, or is abusive, hang up. You are paying for the call. You don't need to accept such a response. Then, don't accept another call immediately. Let your loved one cool down first. When you do accept the next call, explain why you hung up, what you object to, and what kind of responses you are willing to accept. You might be told that you don't understand. There is truth in that, but your loved one doesn't understand your situation either. What is said in anger is often regretted later. By hanging up, you have a chance to clear the air. Arguments happen. It is the disrespect and abuse that aren't acceptable.

If you let children talk, help them prepare what to say and limit their time. Since you are listening on the other side, you can tell what is productive and what is babble. If the children think about this ahead of time and you give them suggestions, their conversations will be more interesting to the loved one.

Try to end a conversation on a positive note. Have a common farewell, a prayer or a blessing, a comment of love or some other special way that is significant for both of you. You might want to save the most special and positive things until last.

• *Be a Writer.* Mail is a great way to keep in touch. If you are a good correspondent, that is wonderful, but if you aren't comfortable writing, look for new ideas. You could start a letter, leave it out for a while, and write a bit from time to time until it feels complete to you. You could clip articles from newspapers and magazines if that is permitted. If not, you could summarize the ideas or write out good quotes to include in the letter. Why not share your daily scripture reading? Share a poem or a part from a book you like.

Buy a bunch of "Thinking of you" cards. These could be crazy, sentimental, traditional, scenic, or some combination of all these. Address and stamp them and then periodically add a quick note and send them one at a time. You could also send postcards. These are cheaper but much more public, so be careful what you say. You don't want your loved one to be teased.

Be sure you send cards for birthdays, anniversaries, and holidays. There are cards available even for unusual holidays such as Halloween, April Fool Day, and Independence Day. You also could have family, friends, or church members send cards and write letters.

If you use a computer, there are great programs available.

You can make your own cards and add crazy graphics and pictures to your letters. If you are artistic, you might make your own cartoons or masterpieces. Be sure to check with the institution to make sure these things are permitted.

Speaking of masterpieces, have the kids make their own. You might have to use colored pencils as some places do not allow crayon, magic marker, glue, or glitter in the facility. Kids usually will be creative with whatever you give them. Have the kids write letters, too. You might have to help them with spelling and ideas in the beginning, but they will soon catch on if this is a regular project. You and the kids could pick a particular day and time to write. This can be a family sharing experience.

If your loved one has poor eyesight or is dyslexic and cannot read, send colorful cards and pictures. Write a few simple words in large print. Print, don't write in cursive. If your loved one has trouble reading but has a friend in the facility, that person might read the letter aloud to help out. Another idea is for you to keep a copy and read it when you next talk to your loved one. The meaning will then be associated with the specific card or letter.

Another idea is to get a book for you and order a copy to be sent to your loved one. You both can read the book, commenting on each section or chapter. Get a joke, puzzle, or riddle book and copy something into each letter. Send the answer in the next letter or laugh together in the next call. Send word search or other puzzles in each letter if that is permitted.

Be sure to comment on an item or two from the last letter your loved one has sent. It's a way to show you read the letter.

Don't forget these letters get opened by staff searching for contraband, and someone on staff also reads them. Be careful what you say so it doesn't get your loved one into trouble.

One way to send something regularly is to subscribe to a magazine for your loved one. Check with the institution to make sure that is acceptable. Ask your loved one what magazine he or she would like. Puzzle magazines also can be purchased in this way.

If you choose to send a book, it might have to be a paperback and probably will have to come directly from a publisher or book store. There might be a limit on the number of books your loved one can keep in a cell, so send books a few at a time. Mail clearance is slow, and it takes time to get the book to the inmate.

• *Be a Visitor.* By visiting your loved one, you are giving a special gift. If you promise to visit, please follow through and do it. It might be best not to promise a particular day or time. If you have a scheduling problem or car trouble, the institution has locked down, or some other issue has developed so that you can't visit, your loved one will be disappointed or worried. It might be better to say, "I plan to come this Saturday or next."

Your visit might be a major project and expense. You will need to plan carefully. Prisons might be several hours' drive from the large cities. In such a case, you might be able to visit only on occasion. You will need a reliable car, especially if you are traveling in bad weather. You also might not wish to travel alone. Perhaps you will meet someone in the visiting area who will travel with you. Sometimes, drivers alternate, or one drives and the other pays for the gas.

In some areas, social-service agencies and other groups such as the Salvation Army provide rides from major cities to prisons. In other places, they might help establish car pools. Some groups drive children and their guardians to see incarcerated parents. If this type of program does not exist in your area, start one yourself or urge an agency, church, or other organization to do so.

If your visit requires overnight accommodations, check ahead to make sure rooms are available. Find the least expensive accommodation, the closest one, a bed and breakfast, or a place on the way. Camping can be another adventure if campgrounds are in the area. In other places, rooms can be rented from individual home owners. Contact a local church to see if someone there can help you. Sometimes there are hospitality houses near institutions that are far away from big cities. Some charge a specific amount, while others accept donations.

Some institutions have Video Visitation capabilities. You can visit over great distances and more frequently. Check with the institution.

Those in Federal Institutions and now large numbers of people from state institutions are moved from state to state. Many people visit loved ones far away from home. Do your homework and research before you travel. Write, call or check the internet for agencies such as those listed in the last paragraph. Call the social-service department of the institution where your loved one resides. Check with the Chamber of Commerce of the city you will be visiting. Seek housing in nearby places, such as suburbs and local towns.

• *Be an International Connection.* If your loved one is incarcerated outside the United States, even for a minor offense, this is a major problem. Contact the State Department and the U.S. ambassador to that country. Contact your senators and representatives. Their offices know the national resources and will help you navigate through the paperwork. The Red Cross and other international organizations and church groups might be of assistance or refer you to resources in that country. Learn as much as you can about these places. No matter what you do, check with the experts before you take any action. You don't want to make matters worse for your loved one. Be careful if you choose to visit. Communication in a different language can lead to misunderstandings and problems. This process will be expensive and could be dangerous.

You should seek a lawyer in the U.S., the other country, or both, and you need to be sure that attorney has expertise in these types of cases. The laws are different in each country. The relationship between the United States and that other country can impact the disposition of the case.

• *Be an Advocate.* The dictionary says that an advocate is one who pleads the cause for another. That means watching what is going on, finding out what should be happening, and finally doing something to intervene if there is injustice.

One way to get information is to actually read all the related statutes that pertain to your loved one's case. Although law books and statutes can be confusing, it is possible for folks without legal training to find and understand the relevant parts of the law. Most law books have an index to guide you to the relevant pages. Use a legal dictionary for any questioned words as they might not have the common meanings. Sometimes, the definition of the words is given in the law or document.

Now, entire law libraries are computerized, which makes researching laws and court cases much easier. You might also find law books in the local libraries. Some cities or counties have law libraries that are open to the public. Colleges and

Universities, especially ones with law schools, also have these materials. Librarians can help direct you to the material you need. Also, ask your loved one's lawyer if you have specific questions.

Sometimes, the criminal justice system is not just. It is a large bureaucracy that has successes and failures. There are many things you can't change. Choose your battles well. Document what you know is wrong. Don't sweat the small stuff. Go for major problems or the most prominent issues. Fight for what will be best for your loved one. If there is a risk of retaliation against the inmate, wait until that person is no longer in a particular facility. Fighting against the system is a slow and methodical process but, in the end, changes can be made. Consider even small changes a victory and keep working toward your goal.

Since institutions are part of local, state and federal government jurisdictions, some changes require changes in the laws. The legal and political processes are changed by legislators or a vote of the people. This can be an expensive and lengthy process. To improve your chances of success, seek like-minded people to join you in your quest for justice and change.

One thing you can do is watch the system and make sure the authorities know you are watching. Don't intentionally cause trouble, but be present when things happen. Showing up in the courtroom is especially important. The judge knows when a family member is present. Go to court when you can.

Remember, each phase of a case has a different focus. Pre-trail, trial, sentencing, and appeals have different requirements. What is needed and works for one part might not fit for another. Learn as much as you can about the law. Keep in mind, however, that is why you have a lawyer who understands the law and the system. Stay in contact with the lawyer.

Especially in the case of appeals, lawyers, family members, and friends have worked for years before turning a case around. In some instances, the case can go all the way to the state's highest court or even the Supreme Court of the United States more than once, and the verdict still might not be changed.

There are organizations that specifically focus on inmate needs, inmate issues and problems in the criminal justice system (The ACLU, for example). It would be wise to connect with such organizations and use their resources and expertise. Some organizations are specific, focusing on just a few issues or one jurisdiction. So, you might choose to join or support more than one. You can get information and assistance from several of them. Use as many resources as you need.

You have political resources also. Let your local, state, and national legislators know the name, case. and jurisdiction, as well as the problems and needs of your friend or family member. This often is handled by staff in the legislator's office, but the legislator will be informed about it. In some cases, these legislators can change the laws or write new laws that impact the situation your loved one faces. Perhaps your inquiries will alter the legislator's point of view in future legislation.

• **Be a Mentor.** The dictionary says a mentor is a faithful counselor. Now, you might not have a degree. You probably don't know all the answers. However, you can be objective, supportive, and honest. You do have more information and resources than you realize.

Be honest! Whatever you do, whatever you say, tell the

truth. That doesn't mean providing every detail, saying whatever is on your mind, or always being assertive. It *does* mean not telling lies and not letting false assumptions stand. Incarcerated people don't trust others and have little reason to do so. They might be manipulative and untrustworthy themselves. Even so, in time, you can gain their trust. You will lose credibility if they learn you are not being honest.

Try to be as objective as you can. This mean looking at the whole picture. The view you get from your loved one is how he or she sees things. You might get a different view from the chaplain, social worker, or people in the administration. Usually the truth is somewhere in the middle. Show your loved one other views. He or she might find them hard to accept at first, but doing this will be helpful in the end.

Also, don't set up false expectations. Your loved one would like you to solve all problems at once. No one can do that. Instead, take things as they come, and do what you can.

One way to avoid false expectations is not to make promises. You can say, "I'll try," "I'll see about it," "I'll investigate," or "I'll take the first steps." *Then do that!* Tell the inmate what you have done and describe the results. The more knowledge you and your loved one have, the better the decisions you can make. Some people ask everyone to do the same thing. By telling what you have done, you can prevent repetition.

If you can be a resource for your loved one, you are giving a gift. When possible, find information. You can ask experts, social workers, and knowledgeable individuals.

• *Be a Spiritual Resource.* You can connect your loved one with his or her own religious resources, but you can also share your own. Sometimes the extended time spent alone provides time for introspection and a time to turn to God. Spiritual sharing needs to be done gently, though. People might not share your beliefs, and sometimes those that do are going through a phase where they are angry with God. While this might lead to evaluations that bring them back to their religious values, if you push too hard, the opposite can be true. Sometimes it is better to be present and not rush.

• *Be an Encourager.* One of the problems for those who are incarcerated, addicted, or involved in negative behavior is poor self-esteem. If you can help your loved one stay active, become involved, be creative, use time profitably, face reality, and make the most of bad situations, you are a true friend. Sometimes just letting people know that you believe in them is enough to give them a more positive outlook on life.

Part VII.
Staying Balanced

THE STORY OF BONNIE AND GRANT

BONNIE KNEW HER SON WAS INTO DRUGS. He had changed so much. He wasn't the clever little kid she and Grant loved so much. He became uncommunicative, surly, pale, and unhealthy. She worried about him for years. Even so, neither she nor Grant guessed the boy would get into this much trouble.

Her stomach churned each time she thought about it. She and Grant hired the best lawyer they could. They weren't poor, although they weren't wealthy either. They had enough to live comfortably in their retirement, which they had planned for a few years from now. They owned a nice home and a new car. They had some money saved up.

After it happened, Bonnie knew her son played some part. She refused to believe, however, that he had committed murder.

Now, she takes his calls from jail. She makes sure he gets mail every day. She checks out anything that might help his case. She seeks advice from people who seem to understand the situation.

Bonnie loves her son. She grieves inside. She puts up a good front. She continues to go to her usual meetings. She still does home sales of cosmetics. Yet she is so frustrated.

Grant brings Bonnie for jailhouse visits, but he waits downstairs. He has visited only once. Grant loves his son and would do anything to change the situation, but he is overwhelmed by anger. How could his son with so much hope and promise do something so stupid? Grant knows he would feel better if he could hit his son just once. He is not an abusive parent or spouse. He is just so angry at this situation.

Grant doesn't want to talk about it. Maybe he can't talk about it. He just stands downstairs and stews as Bonnie visits their son. He will be in the courtroom. If it comes to that, he will go to the prison for visits. He will drive Bonnie to the appellate attorney's office and go in with her, although he will let Bonnie do the talking. He just can't face things right now.

When he's with the guys, Grant just drinks. He doesn't talk.

Most of the time, he works. Every chance he gets, he works. He works overtime. He works on holidays. He stays extra hours. It fills his time. He doesn't have to think.

Bonnie and Grant both love their son. They have different styles of dealing with the issue. They know each other so well after many years of marriage. Each allows the other to work things out in whatever way is needed. They don't compare.

They do share, however. At night, when they are alone together, they talk a bit, but not too much. Bonnie knows words aren't Grant's way. He, on the other hand, lets Bonnie talk through her issues, hoping that will give her peace.

Each of us faces difficulties in our own way. There are different stages we go through. What we are feeling today might change tomorrow as the case unfolds. When something first happens, our reaction could be shock, sorrow, fear, anger, or horror. Then we learn more, and our reactions change. Where we have been afraid, we become angry. Sorrow comes. Then we might get angry again. Some of us get stuck in one emotion and can't get past that.

There is nothing wrong with these emotions. Emotions are necessary. Emotions are good, even when they cause us pain. The problem is not that we have the emotions, but that we don't always know what to do with them.

Try to be sensitive to your own emotions.

WHAT YOU CAN DO FOR YOU

• *Take Care of Yourself.* This is the best advice anyone can give you. If you are going to be a help to your loved one, you must keep yourself in good shape physically, emotionally, and spiritually.

You are under a lot of stress. You didn't create the problem, but you are right there in the middle of it now. Seek positive attitudes and activities that strengthen and fortify you as you face the problems ahead. Some people find comfort in running, others in reading or meditation. Some need to talk to everyone, while others find a single confidant. Develop a strategy that works for you. You have to figure out what fits best in your situation. Try various outlets and shift gears from time to time. Try new things. Fortify yourself for whatever changes will come.

Don't underestimate the physical dimension. Exercise is always important. In times of stress, extra sleep is needed as well. Find ways to stay fit with good nutrition, exercise, and sleeping habits.

You need to take care of yourself one day at a time! That is the best way to help yourself and also your loved one.

• *Maintain Structure in Your Life.* When something

happens that disrupts your life, normal patterns often are destroyed or overridden by the circumstances. If you let yourself get stuck in abnormal emergency patterns and fail to return to normal mode, you will cause yourself too much stress and frustration. You might never return to the old normal, but at least you need to establish a new one. Do this deliberately by looking at what you are doing. If you just let things happen, that increases stress. Choose the most productive and healthy ways to proceed.

Here are some examples of things you can do: 1) return to normal hours for meals, and stop eating fast food so frequently; 2) return to your usual exercise schedule; and 3) join others in planned sports, church, group activities, etc.

• *Keep Yourself Safe.* Stay alert. Even if you believe your loved one is innocent, to have ended up in this position he or she likely has been involved with shady characters. You could be in danger. It is important for you to be more aware of your surroundings. You might avoid going alone to certain places, especially if your loved one's acquaintances will be there.

New locks and alarm systems are ways to keep your home protected. It would be a good idea to change your telephone number and email address as well.

• *Do Not Feel Guilty.* Deep down, you might be having an emotional reaction to these events. You are wondering what you did wrong and how you failed your loved one. Thoughts like that only cause unnecessary suffering. You are not at fault in this. Tell yourself that over and over. Believe it. It is the truth.

• *Watch Out for Signs of Depression.* Depression can be mild or severe. It can be short- or long-term. It can be aggravated by your natural physical systems. Symptoms often include a feeling dullness of life, a lack of energy, extended times of sleep, or lack of appetite. If you recognize any of these symptoms, talk to someone—a good friend, perhaps—about them. If the depression is severe or seems to go on for a long time, seek medical attention. Don't let the problem persist. This is your life at stake.

• *Fill Up Your Time.* Don't leave empty hours in your life. Explore subjects that interest you and are not related to your loved one. You can take courses, read books, attend lectures, check the internet, find others interested in your topic. Also, you should consider starting a new hobby, beginning a sport, or trying out a new exercise program.

• *Create Your Own Support Group.* There are established support groups for families of the incarcerated. People from various social services, churches, and twelve-step programs often can provide you with information and assistance about these.

Those are a good place to start. However, you might want to build a network of friends and associates as well. This will make it easier if you need someone to turn to for help or conversation at a moment's notice.

If the people in your group all have similar situations, you might bring them together for meetings. There, all of you can share your stories and emotions. That helps everyone release tension and find a little peace.

It takes time for groups to build relationships, trust, and friendship. Some people will come and go as their needs change. Some will become the core and continue supporting others for long periods of time. You could be starting something that benefits people for years to come.

If you do start your own support group, one person

should keep the membership list with addresses, phone numbers, and email addresses so meetings can be planned or canceled without difficulty. One person can moderate and lead meetings, or this can be done by a rotation of members. Have an agenda set up in advance so all will know the order of things.

• *Find a Good Balance.* Keep calm. Take care of yourself. Time is a great healer. Even if there are new stresses, you will be prepared to handle them.

• *Have a Life.* Be willing to grow and change, but also allow yourself a little time each day for something you enjoy. This is important. Permit yourself some fun.

Part VIII.
The Spiritual Dimension

THE SPIRITUAL DIMENSION

IN TIMES OF CRISIS, many people turn to God. That is certainly visible in a time of crisis. This is when our relationship with God becomes a reality to us. Just look how many people turned to God and found their way to churches and back to religious observance after 9/11. It is not surprising. We have recognized our own vulnerability and helplessness.

The spiritual dimension of your life is extremely important. We come from different traditions, pray in different styles, use different words, but the concept is the same. God is powerful, and we are not. God is truth, and we are not. God is our strength and protector, our mentor and friend. Each of us has a different view of God. Our theologies also might differ. Our forms of worship vary, but the act of turning to God during our hour of need is common to all religions.

Use the tradition and strength of your church to uplift you in your times of difficulty. Share as much as you can with your loved one. It is a good time to seek God. We need to be reminded that God forgives us and cares for us. Scripture says, "God clothes the lilies and counts the hairs on our head." In both the Old and New Testament, we see healing and care for the poor, the widows, and those in need. This surely is a time of need for you.

Sometimes when negative things happen, we question God. We might become angry with God, the clergy, or other church people because they have not helped. Even if others don't understand, God understands. You still can be connected to God, even when you are upset.

Most clergy are willing to visit or write to your loved one. Sometimes, however, they don't know what to do or say. If that is the case, you might want to find other clergy who understand and can help. Try not to blame people, though, if they are trying to find their way. You don't know what they have experienced in the past.

There is a time for "Fire and Brimstone," for harsh language, and for the reality of sin. That is part of healing, but not the only part. Many people already are filled with guilt. You are entitled to a little guilt. None of us is totally free of responsibility in any situation. It makes no sense, however, to give you all of it when your loved one is the major player. You can have your part of the guilt, but *don't let anyone give it all to you*, even in the name of God.

Some spiritual advisors are wiser than others. A good spiritual advisor will listen and give advice. It is always good to weigh the advice given with the scriptures. If the advice fits the patterns of the scripture, then we can be fairly sure it is true. God also gives us common sense to judge advice. Sometimes we are offered spiritual advice but aren't ready to receive it. It is all right if we are not ready yet. When we get ready, we can look back and try again. We might have needed a clearer vision or some growing time in our own spirituality to accept the advice.

Sometimes we reject advice from advisors because,

although their advice is good and clearly on target, it makes us feel uncomfortable and we refuse to face the issues. On other occasions, advice doesn't quite fit the situation. We must strive for balance in our lives. These decisions are delicate and must be made with consideration and prayer. Since decisions you make impact your loved one and other members of the family, you need to evaluate their needs in reaching your conclusions. You need the whole picture to reach the best possible result.

Family and friends provide one consistent source of help for you. They can reach out and help you if you let them. Of course, use wisdom and check their attitudes before you begin to share deeply. They don't need to agree with everything you think and do to give you wise advice and support. They might not provide more than a listening ear. Even that will help.

Your church is an obvious source of assistance. Presumably, you already have reached out to others in your church. They have been there for you before. Now is the time for them to pray for you and your loved one and to help with the resources of the group.

Join existing groups that work for the betterment of the incarcerated. Find charitable groups that help meet the needs of prisoners and their families. Find profitable ways to fill your time that provide personal satisfaction.

JADA'S STORY

I took a spiritual class about healing many years ago. Jada, the

*class leader, told us a story about her personal journey and gave us
an image that has helped me and others.*

*Jada's father left her mother in the early 1940s. It was hard for a
woman alone with two children. Jada's mother had to work and was
under a lot of pressure. Jada felt sad to see her mother this way, and
she was angry with her father for leaving and not providing child
support. That anger continued for many years. Then, as a middle-
aged woman, Jada had a spiritual awakening and was able to forgive.*

*Jada was a good leader, and I learned a lot from her about
spirituality, healing, and growing closer to God. However, it turns
out that the people in the class helped her as well without even
realizing it.*

*On the last day, Jada shared with us what had happened to her
during the weeks of this class. She knew she was angry at certain
people. She had a problem with doctors who weren't good doctors,
priests who weren't good priests, teachers who weren't good teachers,
etc. While leading the class, she realized that the heart of her issue
didn't have to do with those people, but with fathers who weren't
good fathers. She figured out that she needed to forgive her father
all over again.*

*She told us that healing—or forgiving—was like an onion. You
can take it apart layer by layer. Once you take one layer off, you
might have to wait a while before you can remove the next. For Jada,
the first forgiveness was real. The second, related to our class, was
also real, but it was a deeper healing of the same issue. Now she
knew that she would continue to work at forgiving her father again
and again whenever the time was right and she was ready.*

Jada's story reminds us that some issues are with us for
a long time. For those of you who have loved ones who will
be incarcerated for a lengthy period, you will face both old
and new issues that come to light every day. Sometimes you

will get tired, feel burned out, or grow angry because you are doing your best without it being recognized.

Jada would tell you that you have to have a new look at old realities. She would advise you to take a break, consider the situation in a different way, and count the positive things you have done in the past.

All of us have our low days. All of us feel like crying once in a while. Maybe you need to cry, but then you also need to move on.

Give yourself a break. Take a vacation if you can. Walk in the woods. Read a novel or see a new movie. Have lunch with a good friend. Start a new hobby. Go to a museum. Learn a new game. Do whatever works for you. Hopefully this will prevent burnout.

Sometimes we have negative memories. Something triggers our minds, and we relive the most difficult things we faced. In your case, this might be about your loved one, or it might be about you and your personal experiences. Perhaps looking at this again will give you a new perspective and a better understanding of what is going on in your life as it did for Jada.

DEEPENING AND STRENGTHENING
YOUR INTERIOR LIFE

There are many difficulties, setbacks, and heartbreaks along with the joys and sorrows that come from being a part of any family. To remain healthy and strong we need to foster our interior life. This deals with our personal relationship to our own realities. It connects us with the sacred or holy, which is our attitude toward God (a *Higher Power*, whatever that means to you). It enables us to live according to the philosophy of life we have chosen. It facilitates our interactions with the world.

Some people have deep religious convictions, strong ties with organized religions, family beliefs, religious practices, etc. Others have little or no contact with religious or spiritual training and explanations. For this reason, I have chosen to speak of these areas in a general way, understanding that we are dealing with many different religions or, in some cases, no religion at all.

Look to your own traditions for strength and a path to greater understanding, growth, and a lifestyle that expresses your beliefs. Use the tradition and strength of your church to uplift you in your times of difficulty.

If you have a weak background or are uncertain about your beliefs, then take some time to renew your approach to your Higher Power. Spend time in reading and reflection. Return to your religious roots or study other ways of approaching your understanding of self and the world. Many people have found peace and strength through meditation, discussion, or prayer. Find what works for you.

Spiritual options for your loved one in an incarcerated setting are often limited. Even so, when they have the opportunity, they can choose to participate or not.

The family on the outside is able to seek a source of strength in this area. You have more choices. Even the TV and radio have programs that can inform, direct and enlighten you. Often church groups provide a practical helping community. You need to take the first step and visit those places to see where you feel welcome and where you can grow in understanding, religious spirit and strength.

PRAYERS AND NATURE

Prayer is supplication addressed to God. I like to think of it as talking to God. Sometimes that is formal in a Church, Synagogue, or Mosque. Sometimes we use traditional words of our denomination from spiritual books or sing uplifting songs. Sometimes we have personal prayer that is talking to God one to one. Sometimes even words that are calls for help and understanding, though not traditionally, are prayers.

If this is not your way, find other ways to seek peace. Exercise, music, sharing with others, quiet times of reflection, etc., can help you maintain balance in life.

For many, a connection with nature and the gifts of earth are also a part of our spirituality and a place where we are comfortable in silence and perhaps in prayer. I know people who fish just to be out on the quiet lake, who walk alone in the woods to hear the muted sounds of the creatures, and who climb mountains to praise God from the top. I hope that you have a natural place where you, too, can reflect, even if it is just the view of a tree or flowers or snow from your window.

This reflection brings me to your incarcerated loved one. Some prisons are located in rural areas and have views of nature, but they are the exception. More often, prisons are the most lackluster of all places. Windows are small and high on the wall, only bringing in a little light. Outdoor recreation areas are concrete with metal fencing and surrounded by concrete walls that eliminate the view. People in highly secure units often see only concrete walls, metal, and plastic in dull colors. They can be in those places for years. There is nothing alive except the residents and guards, and maybe a few insects and rodents. Perhaps a bird will fly by on occasion. Even the air is recycled or not moving at all. This is truly a dead environment. If there is any way you can help break up the dullness of your loved one's prison, do so. You will need to contact the administration first, however.

Here are a couple of personal examples:

I managed to get flowers into my jail on Easter. The warden let me leave a few small stems in a paper cup on each pod. My colleagues and I led a short prayer service, but sang only one song since we went to more than a dozen locations. I would then say, "Old teachers never die, and I am an old teacher. Your homework today is to smell the flowers." I gave these tough, hardened guys a task (permission) to smell the flowers, and they did. That was the only day in the year we could do that.

Another experience reminds me of the deprivation of nature that incarceration brings. One facility where I worked had an outdoor enclosed section used only for fire emergencies. A young bunny rabbit managed to get through a small space and into this area. There were some delicious weeds there, and the rabbit was soon too large to leave the way it came in. Of course, the easiest way to deal with this was to kill the rabbit. Even so, the officers working that pod were aware of the fact that the inmates identified with the little rabbit who, in its own way, was now incarcerated. So, one of the officers brought a live-trap and removed the rabbit safely while the inmates watched. I know officers are often criticized, but these guys had an understanding and kindness that was appreciated by all who knew what had happened.

As far as providing a connection to nature is concerned, there is little you can do for your loved one on the inside. Still, try sending a picture of a favorite place, a special view, a tree, a houseplant that has been around for a long time, or the particular type of flower that is in bloom that day. A horticulture book or a magazine with pictures of flowers, plants, or landscapes might work. Pictures of your animals or a book about animal life might be of interest. Also, be sure to share stories about your personal experiences with nature.

One example of this happened to me a few years ago. My cousin, John, who was in his seventies then and died recently, told me this story the last time I saw him:

John rode his bike each morning. One day he came upon a newborn deer in the middle of the road. He stepped away and watched the area, but the mother didn't come back. He knew it wasn't smart to touch wild babies as the mother might reject them, but it also wasn't smart to leave this fawn in the middle of the road. John spoke of picking up this baby, holding it in his arms, and placing it off the road on a pile of leaves. He returned after a while to find that the baby was gone, so he knew that the mother must have come back and cared for it. For John, this was an experience of a lifetime.

I will cherish John's story always. I can picture it in my mind.

If you experience a memorable event, see a special place, or just enjoy an ordinary experience like a walk in the woods, be sure to share it with your incarcerated loved one. Also share a prayer, song, or reading. The two of you can pray or sing together if that works for you.

Since I am a Catholic Sister, I certainly welcome you and promise my prayers for each of you. To me, belief is a gift from God that you can choose to accept. I also believe that things happen in God's time and in God's way. I will pray that you find your path.

Dandelions: A Different View

DANDELIONS

TO MANY PEOPLE, dandelions are weeds. Folks spend time and money to get rid of them or hide them so that they aren't on public display. Society often views inmates like weeds. Money is spent to keep them out of sight.

St. Francis, one of the more well-known of the Catholic saints, didn't see weeds. Instead, he saw flowers.

Dandelions can be beautiful. From green fields, they burst forth in the color of the sun. Often, these make up the first bouquets children give to their parents. These lovely flowers can be fermented into dandelion wine, which lifts the spirit to joy. In the spring, dandelion leaves can be picked and made into delicious salads. You can order one of these radicchio salads in many fine restaurants.

If people we care about are thought of as weeds, we shouldn't just mow them over and forget them. It is our job to help them become the flowers, salad, or wine that they are meant to be.

All of us, like flowers, bloom where we are planted. Dandelions, however, bloom in the most unlikely spots. They are quite hardy and flourish in places roses or tulips would wither and die. Likewise, some people bloom in jails, prisons, inner cities, and other unlikely places. Keep in mind that your loved one might be just such a flower and, if you allow for growth, you will see something amazing and magnificent.

While this is true of your loved one on the inside, it could be true for you outside as well. The dandelion, after all, has a large, strong, useful taproot going deep into the earth. The water of support comes through that root. The root itself makes the plant stand tall. Ask yourself, who or what is the source of the water that nurtures your spirit? Who or what holds you up to help you stand tall?

Dandelions ready to spread their seeds form a white fluffy ball. Like that seed, we are blown into the world to find a place where we can take root and grow. We don't do this alone. Sometimes we join hands and shine together. Wherever we end up, we touch each other.

The dandelion is a gift from God. It is useful, available and beautiful. It reflects simplicity and joy. Whether this is you or your loved one, it should be savored and prized. Work to change your view about the dandelions in your life.

Thank you for all you do for your loved one: your faithfulness, creativity, sharing, and support.

Appendix A
For Professionals
Helping the Incarcerated

THIS BOOK WAS WRITTEN for families and friends. It provides *a basic understanding of the Criminal Justice System* and some of the issues that arise for those it impacts. Other interested parties might include Professionals from related fields: chaplains, social-service providers, medical personnel, volunteers, educators, and students planning for careers that interface with inmates and their families.

SOME TOPICS CONSIDERED:

The Criminal Justice System: Brief overview

The Courts:	General operations and procedures
Incarceration:	Jails and prisons
Reentry:	Needs and cautions
Basis for Problems:	Underlying causes
Families:	Impact, needs, implications, suggested actions

COMMENTS:

1) You will be expected to act professionally, provide the related services, have contact with the appropriate people, and respect the institution and its rules.

2) Keep a positive attitude. Be hopeful and understanding.

3) Even if you know why people are incarcerated, you might not know everything about them. In some cases, a person with a minor charge might be guilty of major crimes for which he or she has not been charged as of yet.

4) Some individuals manipulate the truth to get what they want. You need facts from more than one source to confirm the truth on serious issues.

5) Stick to your own professional expertise and do not enter other areas.

6) Working with the incarcerated is not an easy job. Stay in a good place yourself so you can be helpful to others.

Appendix B
Creating a Support Group

STEPS

1) Determine if there are existing groups in your area.

2) Select a convenient site that is safe, near public transportation, has parking, has handicap access, etc. Libraries, Community Centers, Churches and Agencies often share space.

3) Consider other options, such as phone and video conferences.

4) Choose a member to set dates, calls members, etc.

5) Select a moderator (can be one person or a rotational position) and greeters.

6) Set the general agenda and time frame for meetings.

7) The moderator introduces him/herself, welcomes all attendees and invites them to make a brief introduction.

8) The moderator shares some basic ground rules:

- Start and end on time
- All members are treated with respect, acceptance, and equality
- Confidentiality is essential.

- This is a place of honesty and trust. All are free to share, ask questions, and answer or not.

- Listen carefully, avoid side conversations, and try not to interrupt.

- Don't pass judgement.

- Monitor your participation. Don't talk all the time so that others have a chance to share.

- You are here to support one another, not solve everyone else's problems.

9) Each person shares how things are going, new developments, and any successes or failures.

10) Others are given opportunity to comment.

11) New directions, ideas, topics, and concepts are considered.

12) A closing of some sort (perhaps a short statement or prayer) is spoken.